MAKING ETCHED METAL JEWELRY

Techniques and Projects Step by Step

Ruth Rae & Kristen Robinson

NORTH LIGHT BOOKS
Cincinnati, Ohio
CreateMixedMedia.com

Want even more *Making Etched Metal Jewelry*? How about THREE bonus projects? Maybe you'd like just a little more information on using a jeweler's saw. Would a step-by-step video do the trick? You will find all that and printable templates in the *Making Etched Metal Jewelry* companion page at CreateMixedMedia.com! Just type this address into your browser to get started: **CreateMixedMedia.com/MEMJ-companion.**

Tools and Materials

Used in the Projects and Techniques in This Book

Don't feel like you have to acquire all of these products at once. Start with some quality jewelry tools, supplies for one of the etching techniques, and enough metal, wire and beads for a few of the projects in the first chapter. As you progress through the book, add more unique tools, try out another etching technique and collect items for your materials stash.

THE METAL

- brass sheet metal, 22-gauge
- brass tubing, 14-gauge
- bronze wire, 18-, 22- and 24-gauges
- copper sheet metal, 22-gauge
- gunmetal wire, 22-gauge
- nickel silver sheet metal, 22- or 24-gauge silver wire, 18-, 22- and 24-gauges
- steel wire (annealed), 18-, 22- and 24-gauges

ETCHING TOOLKIT

- acetone or isopropyl alcohol
- baking soda
- cotton balls
- dedicated toothbrush or other soft brush
- eye protection
- ferric chloride
- gloves
- heat gun
- hydrogen peroxide (alternate etching method only)
- mask
- measuring cups
- metal bench block
- muric acid (alternate etching method only)
- plastic-coated tweezers, plastic tongs or wooden chopsticks
- plastic containers with lids (at least 1 for each type of metal)
- protective clothing or apron
- rawhide hammer
- rubber stamps
- Sharpies or other permanent markers
- soft towels (paper towels also work well)
- solvent ink stamp pad
- steel wool

JEWELRY TOOLKIT

- awl
- ball-peen hammer
- bracelet mandrel
- butane torch
- center punch tool
- chain-nose pliers
- dapping set/block
- doming block
- dowels/mandrels
- eyelets
- eyelet setter
- firing block
- flat-nose pliers
- flux
- flux or chemical brush
- mallet
- rawhide hammer
- ring mandrel
- rivets
- round-nose pliers
- screws
- solder
- wire cutters

SAWING KIT

- bench pin
- center punch
- circle cutter
- drill bits
- hand drill or flex shaft
- jeweler's saw
- metal shears saw blades, #2
- rubber cement
- templates
- tin snips
- tracing paper

BEADS & FINDINGS STASH

- bead caps
- clasps
- headpins
- jump rings
- open-back bezels
- preformed bangles, cuffs
- rhinestone chain
- store-bought jewelry chain
- variety of crystal beads, pearls, natural stone beads, metal beads, gemstone beads and charms
- vintage buttons
- vintage pins and brooches

TEXTILES STASH

- embroidery floss
- embroidery needle
- fabric doilies
- fabric dye
- interlining
- scissors
- sewing machine
- suede cording
- tapestry needle
- textile cording
- thread
- variety of fabric pieces and scraps (velvet, muslin, linen, osenberg, felt)
- variety of ribbon (velvet, lace, silk, cotton)

JUMP RING TOOLKIT

- cordless drill (optional)
- dowels
- jeweler's saw (optional)
- sandpaper
- wire, variety of gauges
- wire cutters

SHAPING & FILING KIT

- jeweler's file
- metal file
- sandpaper

RESIN KIT

- craft sticks
- measuring cups (medicinal-type)
- nonstick craft sheet (optional)
- resin kit
- rice (in a bowl)

DARKENING & PATINAS TOOLKIT

- African violet plant fertilizer
- butane torch
- cotton balls
- darkening solution
- firing block
- Gilder's Paste
- gloves
- microcrystalline wax
- plastic container with lid
- protective eyewear
- respiratory mask
- soft cloth or paper towels
- water mister

THE REST

- adhesive
- bone folder
- bookbinding floss
- bowl
- cardstock
- carpet tacks
- clothing iron
- denatured alcohol
- electric griddle
- graphite pencil
- jeweler's glue/adhesive
- ledger paper
- printed transparencies (laser printed)
- printed text
- ruler
- tea bags
- vintage book pages
- vintage photos
- vise or binder clip
- water
- watercolor paper
- wood block

INTRODUCTION

Etching is one of the most amazing and magical techniques you can have in your artistic arsenal. And while some believe etching is intimidating, the truth of the matter is that when it is executed in the correct manner, it is a safe and efficient process. As long as you adhere to all safety guidelines, you are using a relatively straightforward and timeworn alchemist's formula.

There are an array of etching processes to choose from. For this book, we have chosen to focus on the two most frequently used chemical processes. The wonderful thing about etching is the personal signature that is easily added to each piece created. Deep textures, as well as layers of patterns and images, create a virtual landscape of depth.

Etching is the perfect compliment to a variety of jewelry and mixed-media art techniques. For instance, the addition of etched metal and a bit of solder can transform a metal cuff into a masterpiece. One of the most exciting facets of etching is the versatility it affords. While simple chain is a fine option, etched sheet metal is a statement; all that one needs is a pair of sheers and forming pliers to compose a chain created of beautiful etched links.

As you make your way through this etching journey, it is our hope that the projects both encourage you to try the multitude of techniques and inspire you to create your very own projects.

—KRISTEN & RUTH

HOW TO ETCH METAL

While a variety of chemicals and processes can be used to etch metal, we have chosen to focus on the two methods we use the most frequently. In doing so we are sharing techniques that are not only straightforward but also employ the most readily available and safest products.

One of the most important facets of etching is maintaining a safe environment for working in this age-old art. The etching process is covered in detail on the following pages. It is important to adhere to these safety guidelines when etching:

- Always work in a well-ventilated area away from any pilot lights or open flame.
- Wear a mask when etching and during the removal and cleanup process, too.
- Eye protection is strongly recommended.
- Nitrile gloves or other chemical-safe gloves must be worn at all times.
- Protective clothing such as a mechanic's apron will protect your clothing as well as your skin.
- Etching chemicals, including hydrogen peroxide and ferric chloride, must be properly labeled and stored.
- After opening ferric chloride, we suggest placing the closed container in an open plastic bag, as this will prevent spills or drips from coming into contact with any other metal.
- Disposal of etching solution is regulated by each state. Please contact your hazardous waste department to locate your nearest waste roundup facility. DO NOT POUR ANY ETCHING SOLUTION DOWN THE SINK OR SEWER! Seriously. Don't do it.
- When etching, DO NOT mix metals. You must have separate etching solutions and containers for each kind of metal.
- Do not rinse containers or other tools used during the etching process in a stainless steel sink. Doing so may result in etching of the sink.
- Keep pets and children away from your etching area at all times.
- Last but not least, never forget: If it can etch through metal, it can etch through your skin. Use appropriate caution.

The Etching Toolkit

WHAT YOU'LL NEED

acetone or isopropyl
baking soda
brass, copper or nickel silver sheet metal
cotton balls
dedicated toothbrush
eye protection
ferric chloride
gloves
heat gun
mask
plastic-coated tweezers or plastic tongs
plastic containers with lids, 3
protective clothing or apron
soft towels (paper towels also work well)
solvent ink
steel wool
variety of rubber stamps

About the Metal

Within the book we focus on three metals—brass, copper and nickel silver—because these metals can be etched using the least caustic of processes. Each sheet's gauge is chosen for specific reasons (such as the strength of the metal, which is taxed during the etching process). In most cases you can expect to lose the equivalent of two gauges as a result of submerging metal in etching chemicals.

Another important factor when choosing metal to etch is surface. Some manufacturers apply a protective coating to the metal to prevent scratching and tarnishing. It is imperative that you follow the cleaning steps on the following pages in order to remove any surface treatment that might have been applied and which, if not removed, will negatively impact the etching process.

The size of the sheets of metal we work with for the projects in this book vary. Generally we use 4" × 4" (10cm × 10cm) pieces of metal. You can use larger pieces—you may have more cutting to do. The ***She Dreams Journal*** (page 112) requires slightly larger pieces of metal—6" × 6" (15cm × 15cm) should do it. You can also use leftover scraps of etched metal in many (most) projects. Feel free to mix and match metals to suit your needs and preferences.

Brass Sheet Metal: 22-gauge brass sheet metal is preferred. The primary reason for choosing this gauge is durability during etching. A deep etch is achieved, while at the same time, the metal holds up well and recovers from manipulation.

Copper Sheet Metal: 22-gauge copper sheet metal not only etches deeply but it also possesses good durability and longevity.

Nickel Silver Sheet Metal: 22- or 24-gauge nickel silver can be etched with great results.

Brass Tubing: Brass tubing is generally composed of 14-gauge metal. Because the metal is composed of more layers of heavier metal, it may take a bit longer to achieve the desired etch. It is imperative that you properly clean both the inside and the outside of the tubing.

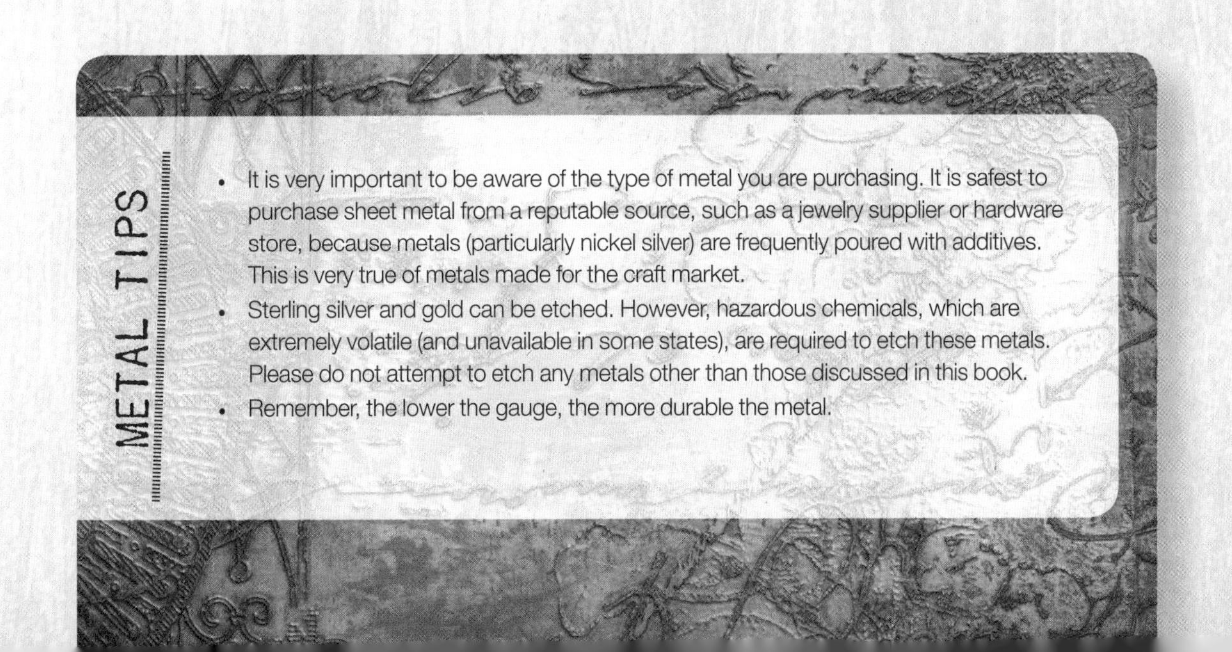

METAL TIPS

- It is very important to be aware of the type of metal you are purchasing. It is safest to purchase sheet metal from a reputable source, such as a jewelry supplier or hardware store, because metals (particularly nickel silver) are frequently poured with additives. This is very true of metals made for the craft market.
- Sterling silver and gold can be etched. However, hazardous chemicals, which are extremely volatile (and unavailable in some states), are required to etch these metals. Please do not attempt to etch any metals other than those discussed in this book.
- Remember, the lower the gauge, the more durable the metal.

Etching Metal With Ferric Chloride

Ferric chloride is the most popular etching solution. It can be purchased from jewelry suppliers, chemical companies and art stores. When left in its natural state (with no water or baking soda added), the acid produces almost no fumes. It is important to note we only purchase ferric chloride in a liquid state.

Preparing the Metal for Etching

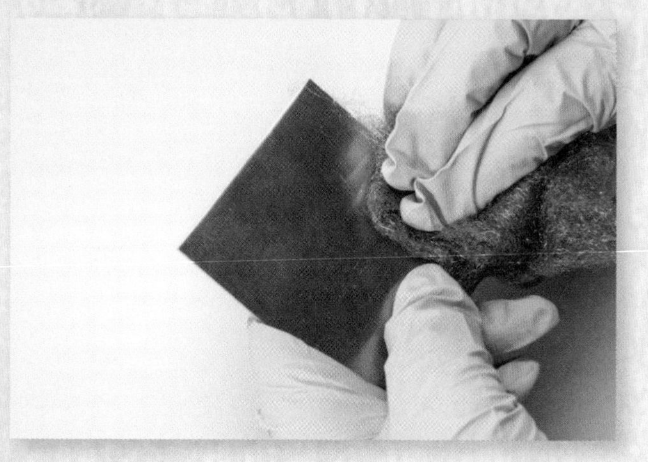

1 Saturate a cotton ball with acetone or isopropyl (rubbing) alcohol. Rub the cotton ball over the metal. Be sure to rub all parts of the metal—both sides and the edges. Always wear gloves to protect your hands, and wipe the metal with a soft towel to dry it—there is no need to rinse.

2 Scrub the metal with steel wool and wipe with a soft towel.

Applying Ink to the Metal

1 Use a solvent ink—StazOn works especially well. Saturate your stamp by pressing the ink pad onto it.

2 Press the stamp onto the metal.

3 Layer on additional stamping as desired. Text and images work equally well.

4 Dry the ink with a heat gun if desired—doing so speeds up process.

TIPS
ALTERNATE INK APPLICATIONS

- You can also write or draw on metal with a Sharpie marker—the results will be just like those achieved with an ink pad and stamp.
- If the surface of the metal you will work with is curved—like a cuff bracelet—apply the metal to the stamp and roll it back and forth until your have the desired coverage.
- You can ink up tubular surfaces in the same way—roll the tube over the surface of the stamp.
- You can also add images using heat. This works especially well with photos, and you can see how to do this step-by-step in *Beholding the Past Photo Wrap Bracelet*, page 78.

Etching the Metal With Ferric Chloride

1. Prepare your work area for etching. With gloves on, fill a plastic container with ferric chloride (etchant solution).
2. If you want to etch both sides of the metal, create a slight bend in the center as this will allow the metal to fall away and create a nice etch. Place the metal in the solution. Place the lid on the container and leave the metal in the solution for thirty minutes.
3. Gently agitate the container of solution every ten minutes by lifting and tilting.
4. Check the progress of the etching at about thirty minutes. Use chopsticks to lift the metal and assess whether the metal is etched as you desire. Make sure you use chopsticks or a similar implement made of wood because metal will react in the solution and any metal you use may become unintentionally etched. (You can use plastic-coated tweezers or tongs if you'd like.) If you want a stronger, deeper etch, return the metal to the solution and check it at five-minute intervals. But be aware that if the metal is allowed to etch too long, it will become thinner, weaker and inappropriate for some projects.

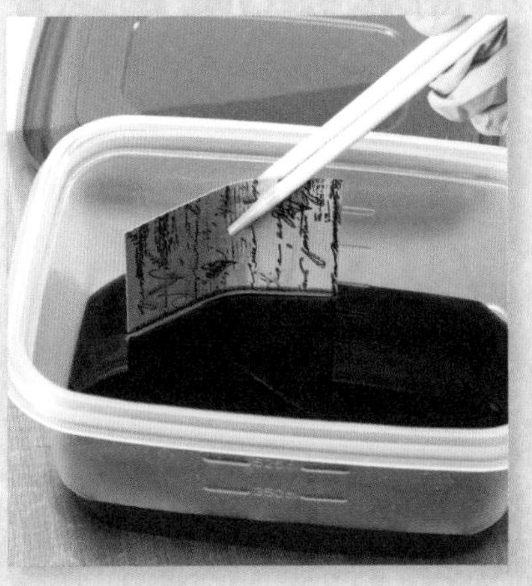

Removing the Metal From Etchant

1 Remove the metal from the etchant and rinse off the etchant by swishing the metal around in a plastic container of water.

2 Fill another plastic container with baking soda. Place the metal in the container and cover it with baking soda to neutralize the etching solution.

3 Lift the metal from the baking soda and brush it with an old toothbrush to remove any etchant residue.

4 Rinse the metal again in the container of water.

Cleaning, Drying and Reshaping the Metal

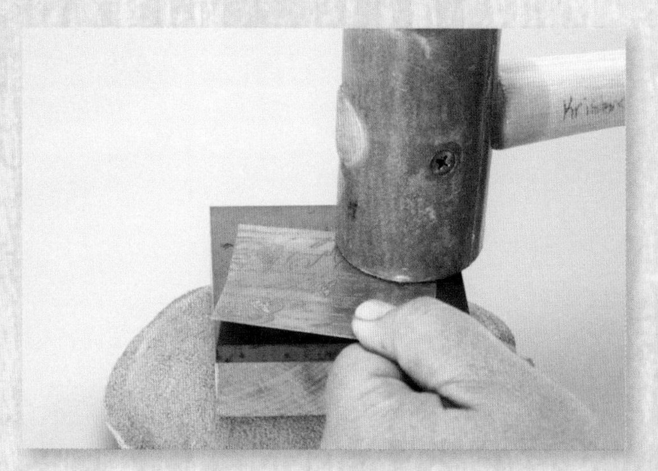

1 Dry the metal using a soft cloth or paper towel. Then, using steel wool, buff the metal. This will bring out the etching and remove any lingering residue.

2 Place the metal onto a metal bench block and reshape it using a rawhide hammer. Tap gently but firmly. Hammering with rawhide reshapes (and maintains the integrity of the etching). Hammering with metal strengthens (or hardens) the metal and blurs the etching.

Etching Metal With Muric Acid and Hydrogen Peroxide

Etching metal with muric acid and hydrogen peroxide is an alternative if you are unable to locate ferric chloride. Muric acid is composed of chemicals primarily used to clean pools, and a pool supply store is the most common location from which to purchase this chemical. It is very important to note that *this process is much more caustic and aggressive in terms of fumes and chemical reactions* than the ferric chloride process.

When using this combination, you will find the first two batches of etching you do will process very quickly, sometimes in less than ten minutes. After two batches, the solution diminishes in strength and the time it takes to etch will increase. Again, you must dispose of this solution properly while adhering to your state's hazardous waste laws. Please also follow the safety guidelines outlined on page 8.

1. Prepare your work area for etching: With gloves on, fill a plastic container with two parts muric acid and one part hydrogen peroxide.
2. Place the metal in the solution. Place the lid on the container and leave the metal in the solution for ten minutes.
3. Gently agitate the container of solution every five minutes.
4. Check the progress of the etching at about fifteen minutes: Use chopsticks to lift the metal and assess whether the metal is etched as you desire. Make sure you use chopsticks or a similar implement made of wood for this step because metal will react in the solution and any metal you use may become unintentionally etched. (You could use plastic-coated tweezers or tongs for this step if you'd like.)
5. If you like the etching, remove the metal from the etchant. Otherwise replace the metal back into the solution and check progress every few minutes.

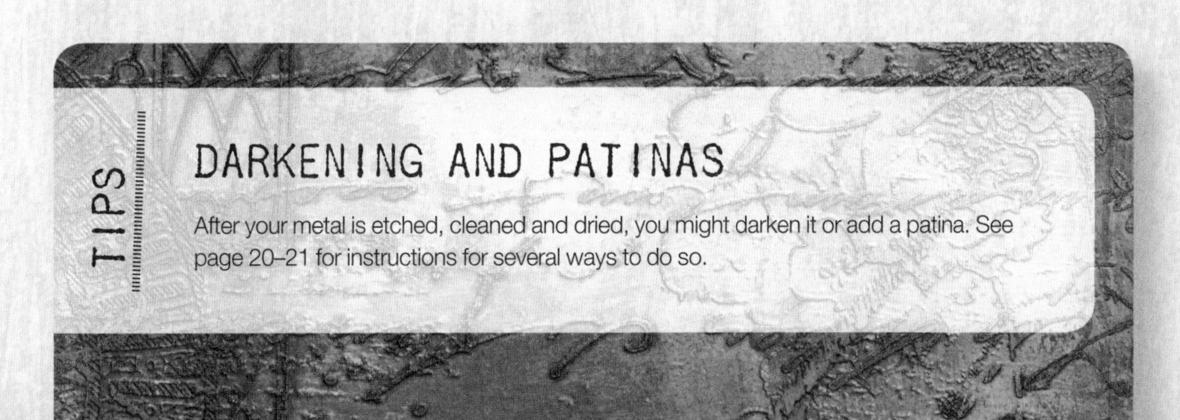

TIPS

DARKENING AND PATINAS

After your metal is etched, cleaned and dried, you might darken it or add a patina. See page 20–21 for instructions for several ways to do so.

JEWELRY TECHNIQUES

The tools we chose to use when creating the projects in the book are not only versatile but are used on a consistent basis and in many cases can be used for more than one technique. When investing in tools, it is important to evaluate what you wish to achieve (and a good set of ergonomic pliers is a must).

The Jewler's Toolkit

WHAT YOU'LL NEED

- ball-peen hammer
- bracelet mandrel
- butane torch
- center punch tool
- chain-nose pliers
- dapping set/block
- doming block
- dowels/mandrels
- eyelets eyelet setter
- firing block
- flat-nose pliers
- flux
- flux or chemical brush
- mallet
- rawhide hammer
- ring mandrel
- rivets
- round-nose pliers
- screws
- solder
- wire cutters

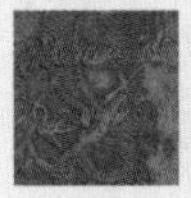

Making Jump Rings With a Drill

This is a wonderful technique to have in your creative arsenal as you become more adventurous in designing your own jewelry. You can make jump rings anytime with the gauges and colors of wire that fit your piece. If you want to make a large number of jump rings in a short amount of time, a drill is a convenient tool to have.

Jump Ring Toolkit

WHAT YOU'LL NEED

- cordless drill (optional)
- dowels
- jeweler's saw (optional)
- mandrel
- wire cutters
- wire, variety of gauges and metals

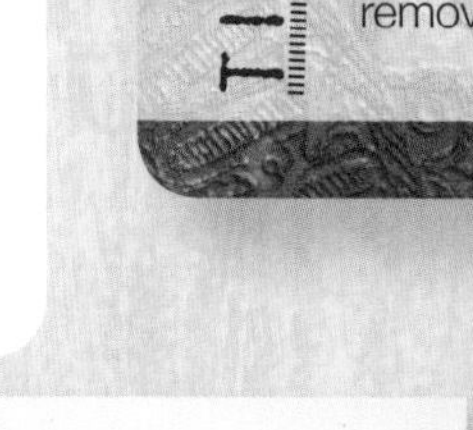

TIPS

When using steel wire, sand the wire first to remove the finish; this will create an aged look.

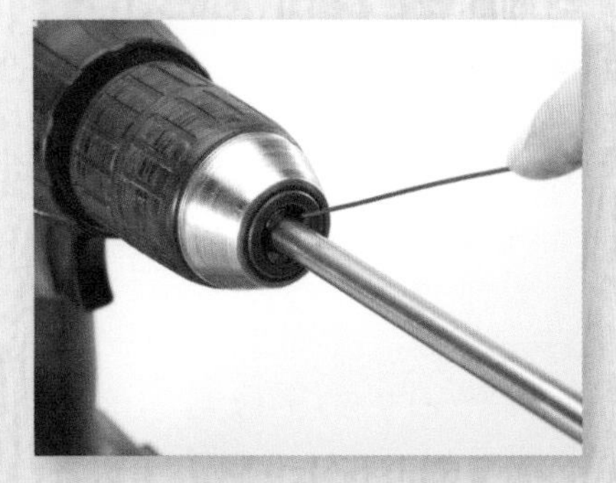
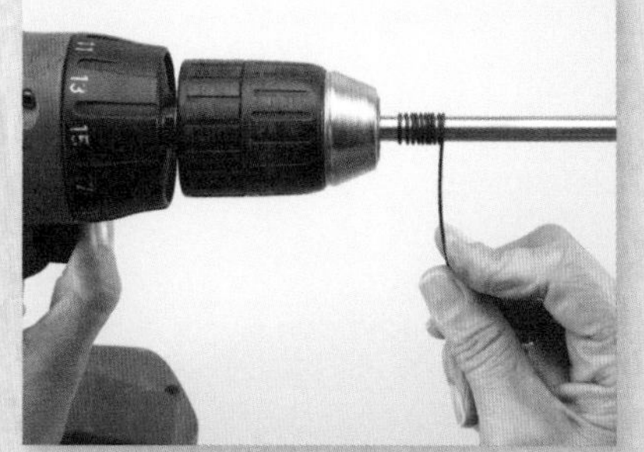
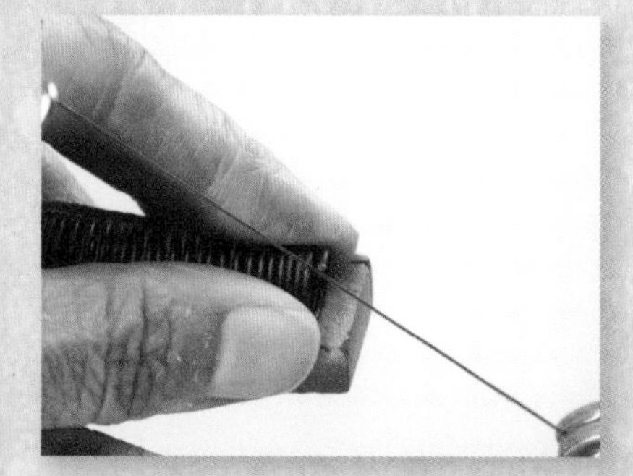

1 Cut 1" (30cm) of steel wire. Insert the wire and the dowel into the drill and tighten to close.

2 With the drill on low, wrap the wire around the dowel creating sixteen jump rings.

3 Remove the dowel and wire from the drill. Slide the coiled wire off the drill. Using the jeweler's saw, cut the rings apart from one another. Wire cutters can also be used to cut apart the rings; however, a saw will produce the cleanest cuts.

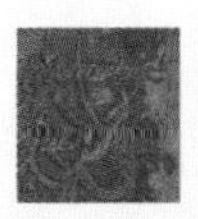

Opening and Closing Jump Rings

Properly opening and closing jump rings ensures your jewelry will stay connected. Never distort the shape of the jump ring; it should always maintain a circular shape.

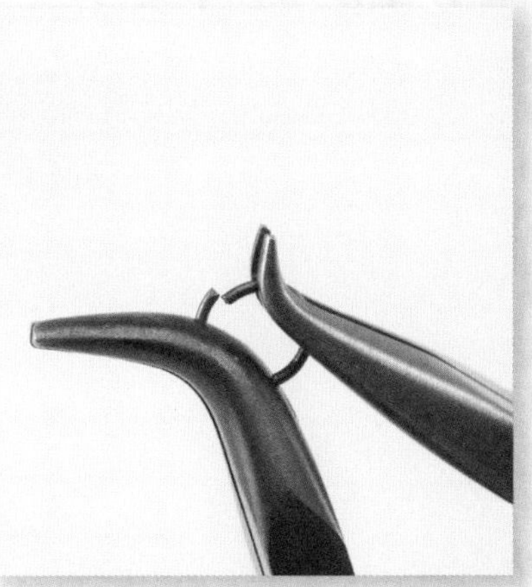

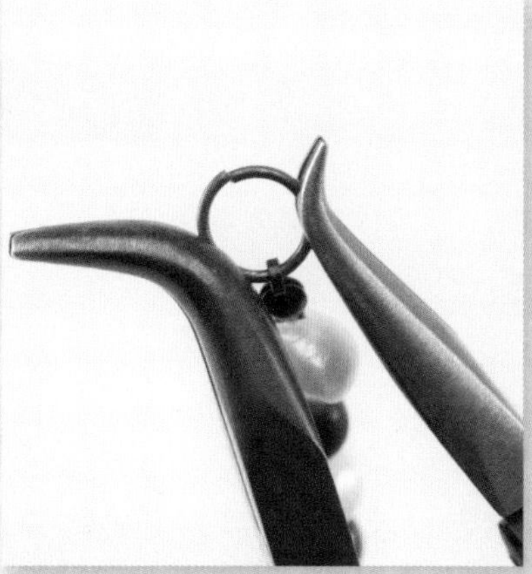

1 Using two pairs of pliers, grip the jump ring on either side of the cut. Using a scissor motion, open the jump ring.

2 Slide on any desired objects.

3 Close the jump ring by gripping it as you did in step 1 and bring the cut ends back together.

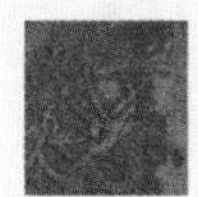

Turning a Loop

This technique allows you to make quick connections for links and dangles.

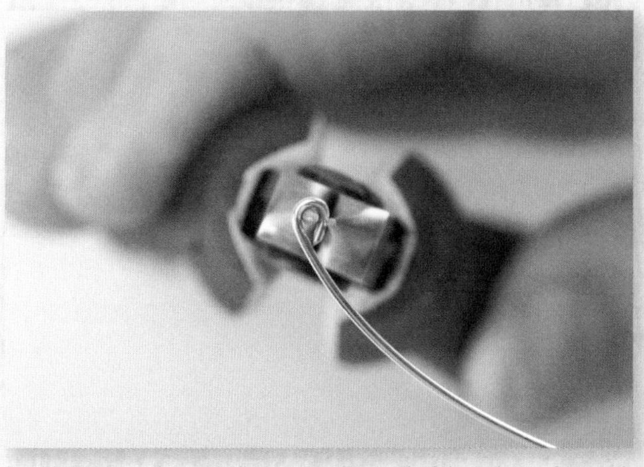

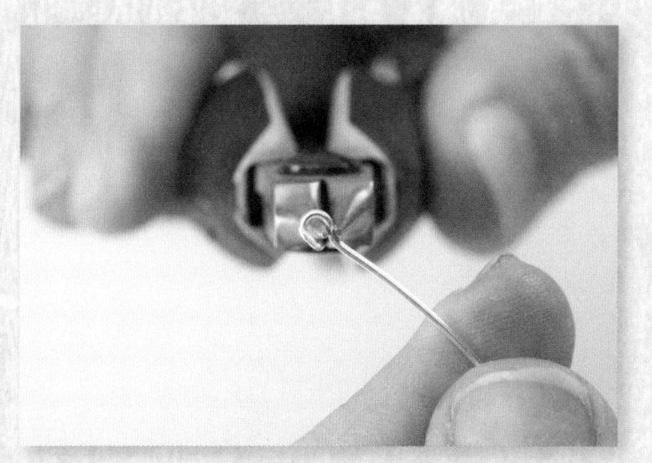

1 Using round-nose pliers, turn the end of the wire to form a loop.

2 Straighten the loop on the wire by placing the round-nose pliers behind the loop and bend the loop up slightly.

Making a Wrapped Dangle

Wrapping dangles is a great alternative to making simple loop dangles, and wrapping is also a more secure option.

1 Thread a bead onto a headpin.

2 Using round-nose pliers, turn the wire around the jaws to form a loop.

3 Wrap the wire tail around the base of the wire loop.

4 Trim any excess wire.

Making a Wrapped Link/Wrapped Link Chain

Sometimes a design needs a little more strength and visual heft; the wrapped link is perfect for such occasions.

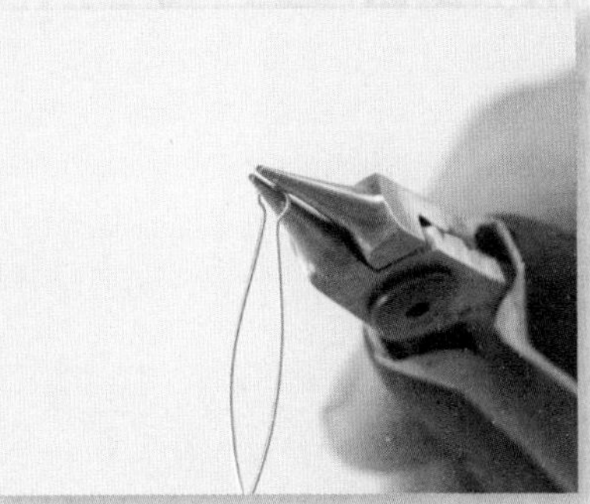

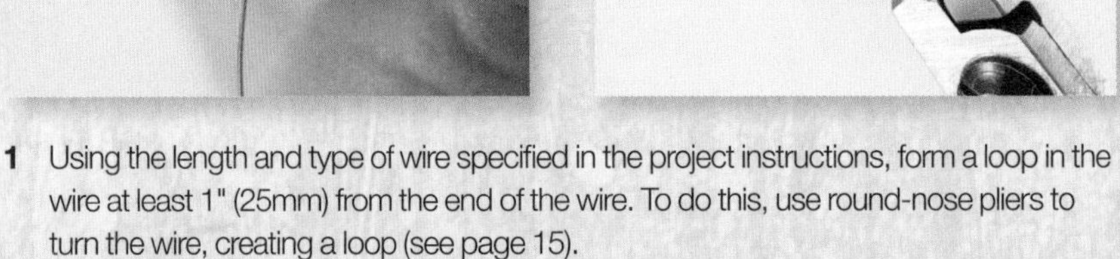

1 Using the length and type of wire specified in the project instructions, form a loop in the wire at least 1" (25mm) from the end of the wire. To do this, use round-nose pliers to turn the wire, creating a loop (see page 15).

2 Wrap the tail around the loop. Trim the excess wire.

3 Thread a bead onto the wire. Repeat steps 1–2 to complete the link.

4 Repeat step 1, this time threading the wire through the loop of the previous link before wrapping.

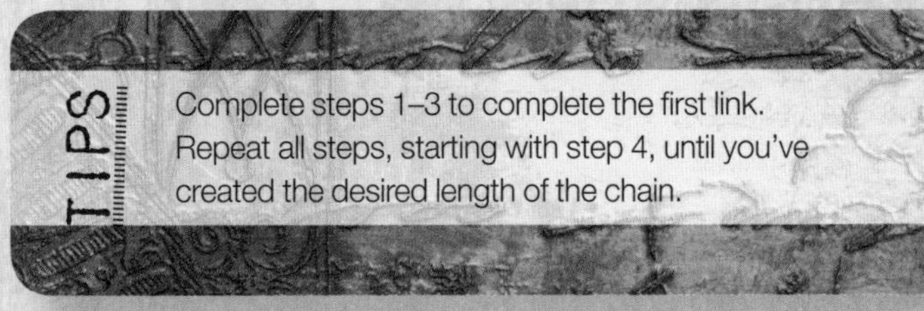

TIPS

Complete steps 1–3 to complete the first link. Repeat all steps, starting with step 4, until you've created the desired length of the chain.

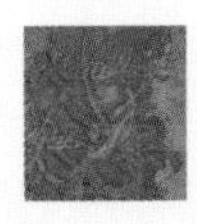

Making a Hook/Clasp

A simple hook clasp is a great alternative to using purchased clasps: Not only does it add another layer of creativity to your piece, it also allows for a personal touch as well as continuity in metal.

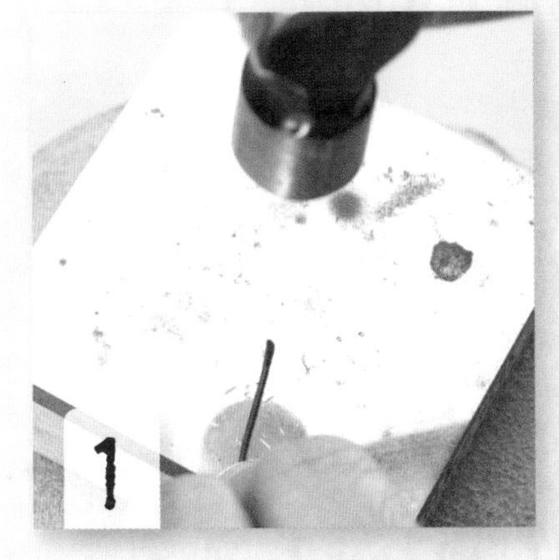

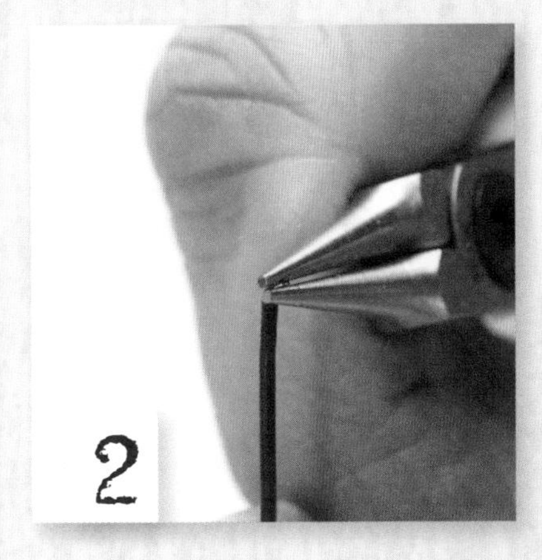

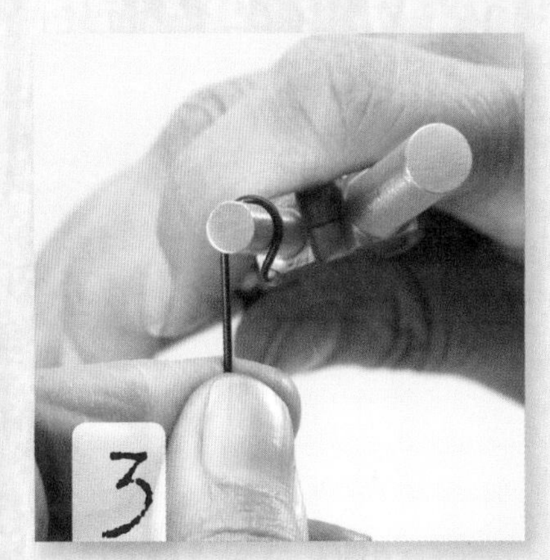

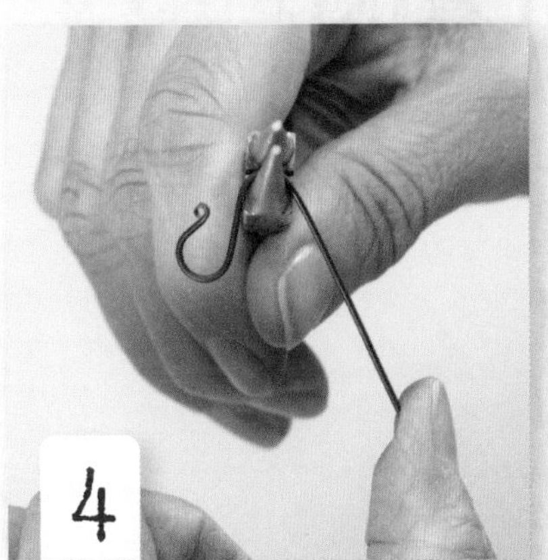

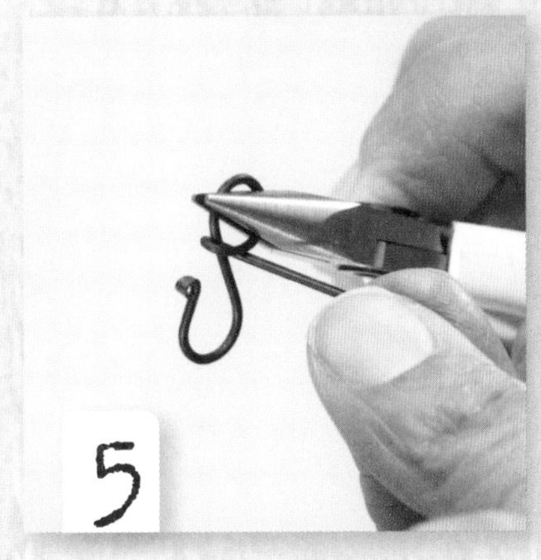

1 Cut a 4½" (11cm) piece of 18-gauge wire (you can use a higher gauge if you'd like). Hammer one end to make a small paddle.
2 On the paddle end of the wire, use round-nose pliers to turn a very small loop.
3 Wrap the wire tail around a ½" (13mm) dowel or cylinder and in the opposite direction of the last loop.
4 Make another loop in the wire.
5 Wrap the wire around the neck of the wire, between the two larger loops.
6 Trim any excess wire.
7 Hammer flat the curve near the open end of the clasp. Do the same with the curve of the closed part of the clasp.

Using a Circle Cutter

Perfect circles are by no means impossible to achieve with a jeweler's saw. However, with the addition of a circle cutter to your tool arsenal, perfect circles are achieved each and every time and with relative ease. Look for a circle cutter that is of good quality and that includes versatile sizes.

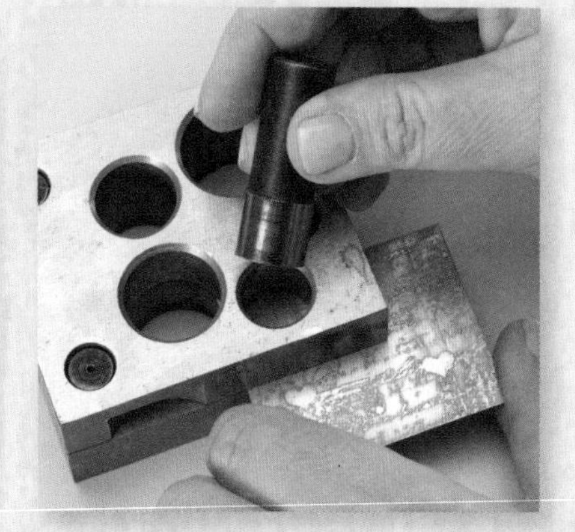

1. Line up sheet metal to fill the hole for the size of the circle you wish to cut.
2. Insert the punch rod into the appropriate hole of the circle cutter.
3. Hammer away! You may have to use a good amount of force, but eventually the circle will fall free of the circle cutter.

Using a Dapping Block/Doming a Circle

The addition of a dapping and/or doming block to your toolbox is a must. Simple circles can easily be transformed into domed beauties, perfect for charms, clasps, bead caps or anything you can dream up.

1. Place a metal disc into a hole that measures about twice its size.
2. Using a dapper and hammer, hammer the disc until it begins to form a cup, moving the dapper in a circular motion as you work.
3. Once the disc begins to dome, switch to a smaller dapper and keep the disc in the same hole.
4. Once the sides of the disc begin to cup towards the top of the hole, move the disc into a smaller hole and repeat the process until the disc is cupped as desired.

Using a Jeweler's Saw

A jeweler's saw creates an atmosphere of ease when faced with challenging cuts. Not only does the saw create clean cuts that eliminate the need for a lot of filing, it is also perfect for cutting curves and tight areas.

1 After using the saw to cut a shape from a larger piece of metal, drill a hole in the center of the shape.

2 Attach a bench pin to a sturdy table or surface. Release one end of the blade from the saw and run it up through the back of the hole. Place the blade back into the frame and close.

3 Begin cutting the center away, keeping the saw perpendicular to the floor.

4 Remove the cut metal. (Remove the template paper, and file rough edges if need be.)

TIPS

- Visit **CreateMixedMedia.com/MEMJ-companion** to watch videos that demonstrate everything you need to know about using a jeweler's saw.
- Always ensure your blade is tight within the frame, as a loose blade will not cut and will likely break.
- Adding beeswax to your blade will ensure a smooth cutting action.

Darkening and Adding Patinas

Darkening metal and/or adding a patina is a fantastic way to bring out the layers of etched metal. The process of adding darkening solution not only allows the layers of etched metal to come to the forefront but also creates such an amazing level of depth in just a handful of minutes. Creating a patina with Gilder's Paste creates layers of color as well as depth, kicking your piece up to a whole other level.

If you wish to step things up a bit, creating a patina with a torch is not only exciting but you'll see different results each and every time. And we would be remiss if we did not introduce you to the process of etching with plant fertilizer. While this process creates amazing magnitudes of color, it does require a bit of patience Be assured the wait is well worth it!

Remember, always wear gloves when working with any type of patina process.

Darkening Solution

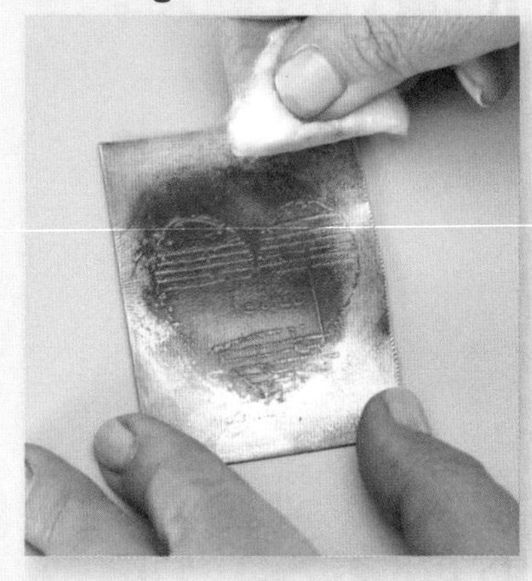

To darken the metal:

1 Place a cotton ball into a darkening solution (such as Jax).

2 Wipe the solution onto etched metal and allow it to remain until the metal turns the desired color (in most cases, black).

3 Dip the darkening metal into a tub of water to remove any excess solution.

4 Dry the metal with a paper towel.

5 Buff the metal with steel wool until the etched portions appear darker than the background.

Gilder's Paste and Microcrystalline Wax

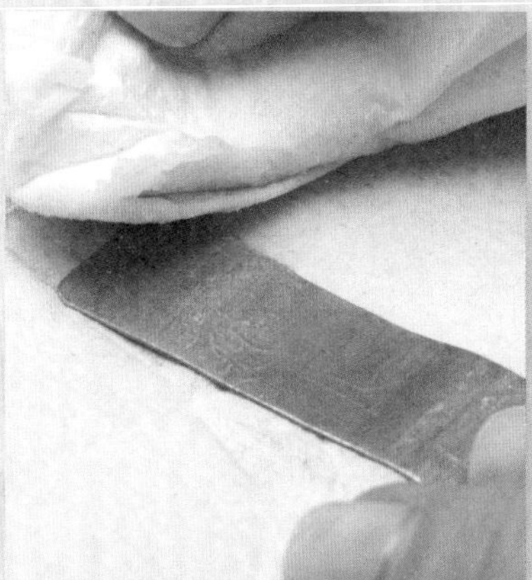

1 Using a paper towel or soft cloth, apply Gilder's Paste to the metal. Apply multiple layers but allow each layer to dry before adding the next.

2 With a paper towel or soft cloth, apply microcrystalline wax over the dried Gilder's Paste. The wax will act as a sealant. Allow the metal to cure prior to handling. (We recommend and use Renaissance brand microcrystalline wax.)

Heat Patina

1 Place the sheet metal on a firing block. With a butane torch, heat the metal slowly. Stop periodically to check the color and stability of the metal. Moving the torch in slow circles, continue firing until the color you desire is achieved. Let the metal cool for at least ten minutes. (This is very important—no shortcuts!)

2 With a soft cloth, add a layer of microcrystalline wax. Allow the wax to dry, and add two more layers of wax, allowing drying time after each.

NOTE

The heat patina process will typically produce different results each time it is used. The copper will change colors as you heat it, and the results will range from gold to orange to pink and purple to midnight and light blue and then to black.

Plant Fertilizer (for African Violets)

It may seem odd to introduce plant fertilizer into the process of metal etching, however, the patina the plant fertilizer produces is amazing. We promise. (We use Miracle Grow for African violets when we patina with the process.)

1 Bend the etched sheet of copper slightly and put it in a plastic tub or container. Drip African violet fertilizer onto the copper in a random pattern.

2 With a cotton ball soaked with African violet fertilizer, rub both sides of the copper.

3 Mist the copper with water.

4 Close the container and allow the patina to process.

5 The processing should be complete after about three days, but you can remove the copper anytime you've achieved the color you desire.

6 Take the copper out of the container and preserve it by rubbing the piece with microcrystalline wax.

SAFETY TIPS

WORKING WITH PLANT FERTILIZER

Always wear gloves when handling plant fertilizer. It is also a good idea to wear a mask and eye protection and to use this process only in a well-ventilated area. Be aware of manufacturers' cautions!

1 BEGINNING THE ETCHING JOURNEY

As you begin your etching journey, you will be introduced to an array of etching techniques as well as new and inventive jewelry techniques. What might appear as a simple piece of copper sheet metal is quickly transformed into a miniature book cover that houses a plethora of beautiful antique papers and hand-dyed lace. Etched nickel silver is quickly amped up with the addition of Gilder's Paste, and three simple bangles come together to create a stacked story.

Chapter 1 will introduce you to many tools that make the process of creating etched metal jewelry much more fun and, frankly, easier. From bench blocks to circle cutters to dapping blocks, be prepared to let your imagination run wild while hammering away.

So gather your tools, some favorite beads and baubles, and a few sheets of metal, and prepare your work environment. We are about to embark on the creative journey of a lifetime.

ETCHED BANGLES

Simplicity is the most elegant of styles. While these bangles are interesting on their own, they create an intricate story when stacked—one that perhaps only the wearer is truly aware of. Handwritten odes combined with markings are nestled within the channels of each bangle in an almost secret manner—a perfect project to practice etching your own words and images.

WHAT YOU'LL NEED

METAL, ETCHED AND RESHAPED:
channeled bangle bracelets, ¼"(6mm), 3

nickel silver, 22-gauge, 2 scrap pieces

OTHER METAL:
bronze wire, 24-gauge

headpins, 2

jump ring, 10mm, 18-gauge

JEWELRY TOOLKIT:
center punch

flat-nose pliers

forming pliers

SHAPING & FILING TOOLKIT:
metal file

BEADS & FINDINGS STASH
briolette crystal, 12mm, 1

coin pearl, 12mm, 1

turquoise bead, 9mm, 1

SAWING KIT:
circle cutter

drill and 1/16" bit

metal shears

wood block

DARKENING & PATINAS TOOLKIT:
Gilder's Paste, green

microcrystalline wax

paper towels

FABRIC & SEWING STASH:
scissors

silk ribbon, pale peach, 6" (15cm)

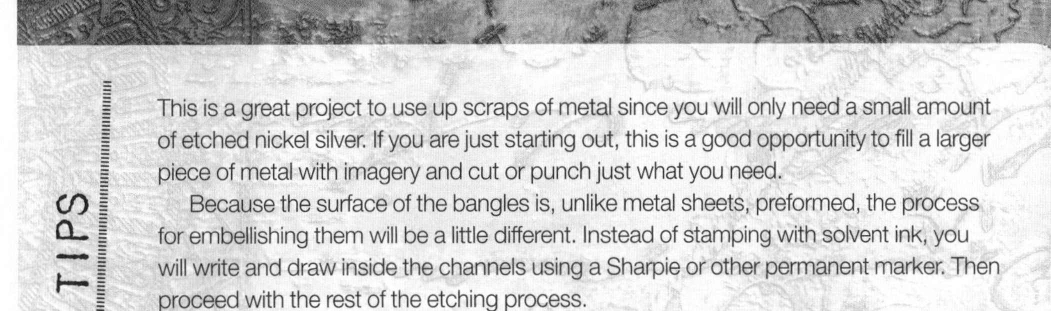

TIPS

This is a great project to use up scraps of metal since you will only need a small amount of etched nickel silver. If you are just starting out, this is a good opportunity to fill a larger piece of metal with imagery and cut or punch just what you need.

Because the surface of the bangles is, unlike metal sheets, preformed, the process for embellishing them will be a little different. Instead of stamping with solvent ink, you will write and draw inside the channels using a Sharpie or other permanent marker. Then proceed with the rest of the etching process.

1 Cut Metal and Mark Holes
Using metal shears, trim one piece of etched nickel silver to 1½" × 2½" (4cm × 6cm) to form a bar. Using a marker, mark a drilling guide on each end of this piece.

2 Create Guides and Drill Holes
Using the marked guides, a center punch and wood block, create a guide for the drill bit. Then drill holes using a 1⁄16" drill bit.

3 Round Edges
Snip all four corners of the bar piece. Using a metal file, file all corners until they are rounded.

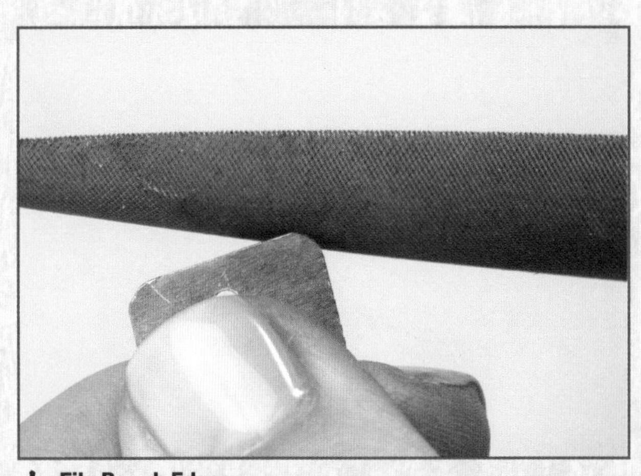

4 File Rough Edges
File any rough or sharp edges that remain. File the metal only in one direction, as moving the file back and forth in a sawing-type motion can sharpen the edges. It is always best to file downward away from your body.

5 Add Patina
Using a soft cloth, apply Gilder's Paste to the bar. (See *Darkening and Adding Patinas*, page 20.)

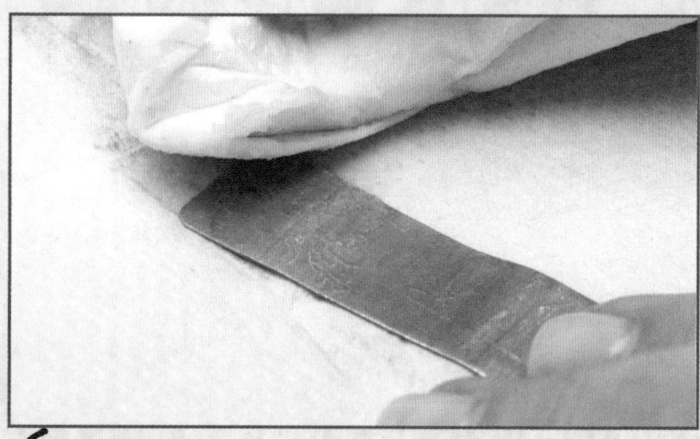

6 Seal With Wax
With a paper towel apply a layer of microcrystalline wax to the bar. (See *Darkening and Adding Patinas*, page 20.)

7 Create Attachment
Using 3mm forming pliers, create a bend in the bar, ½" (13mm) from one end.

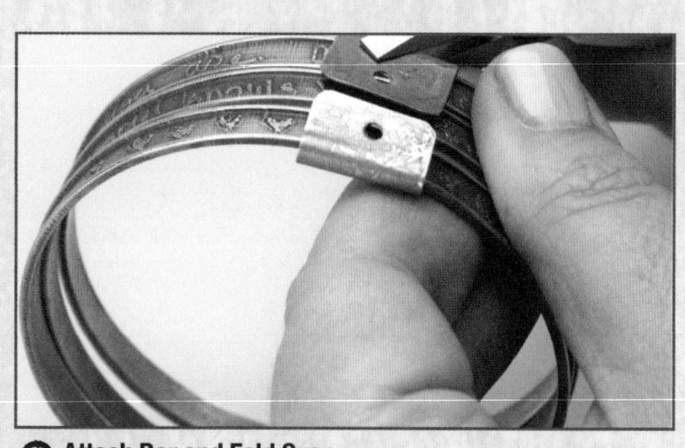

8 Attach Bar and Fold Over
Place the bent bar over the bottom of the three bangles. Crimp with flat-nose pliers if needed.

As you did in step 7, create a second bend to secure all bangles and fold it over to secure the bangles within the bar.

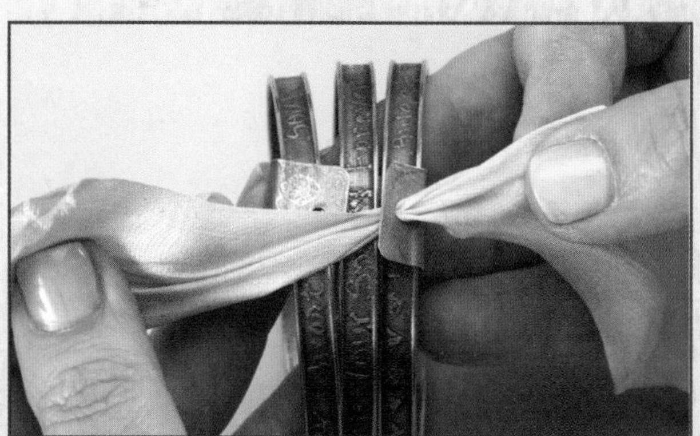

9 Attach and Fasten Ribbon
Through one drilled hole insert one end of the silk ribbon. Slide the other end of the ribbon through the other hole, and tie the ribbon ends together.

10 Create Disc Bead
Using the remaining piece of etched nickel silver and a circle cutter, create a ¾" (19mm) disc (see *Using a Circle Cutter*, page 18).

As you did in steps 5 and 6, add patina and microcrystalline wax to both sides of the disc.

Using a drill with a ⅟₁₆" drill bit, drill a hole at the top of the etched disc.

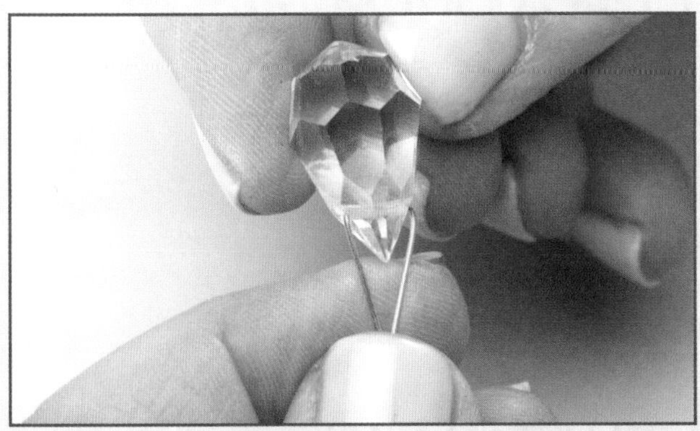

11 Create Crystal Dangle

Cut a 6" (15cm) length of 24-gauge bronze wire. Place the wire through the crystal.

12 Wrap Wire

Pull both ends of the wire up. Fold one end of the wire down and wrap it around the other end. Trim any excess wire from this wrap.

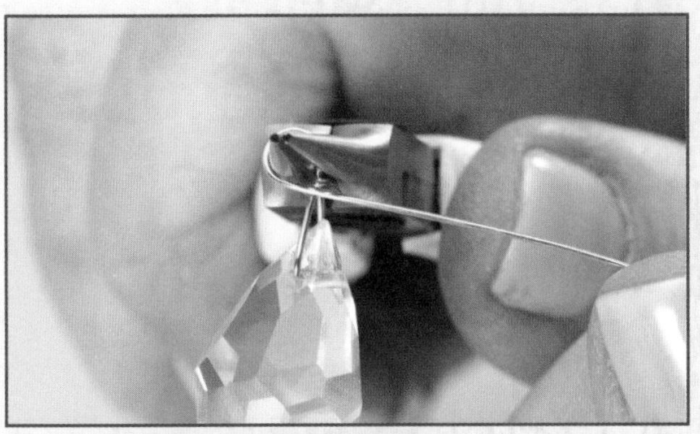

13 Create Loop and Bead Dangles

With round-nose pliers, create a wrapped loop at the top of the crystal, then trim any excess wire (see *Making a Wrapped Dangle*, page 16).

Onto one headpin, place a coin pearl and then wrap the headpin into a dangle. Place the turquoise bead onto the other headpin and wrap it into a dangle.

14 Attach Jump Ring and Complete Closure

Open a 10mm steel jump ring, place the disc and three bead dangles onto it, and then close it (see *Opening and Closing Jump Rings*, page 15).

Slide the closed jump ring with dangles onto the ribbon and tie the ribbon into a double knot.

THE STORY AS TOLD NECKLACE

There is something fascinating about old books and the tales held within them. Creating your own book with metal you have etched and antique book pages, dyed lace and perhaps a bit of secret journaling is more than fulfilling. "Exciting" is an even better way to describe it, for at the end of the day you are truly the only one who knows what lies within the pages of this tiny hand-crafted tome. In this project you'll also make a beautiful and unique bale by cutting etched brass tubing.

WHAT YOU'LL NEED

METAL, ETCHED AND RESHAPED:
brass tubing, 3⁄8" (9mm)

copper, 24-gauge, 1" × 3" (25mm × 8cm)

OTHER METAL:
brass headpins, 1

brass rolo chain, 4mm, 14" (3½cm)

gunmetal wire, 22-gauge

jump rings, 5mm, 1

silver chain, 10mm, 3½" (9cm)

silver headpins, 1

silver wire, 22-gauge

steel wire, annealed, 24-gauge

JEWELRY TOOLKIT:
flat-nose pliers

forming pliers

round-nose pliers

wire cutters

SAWING KIT:
drill and 1⁄16" bit

jeweler's saw and #2 blade

metal shears

SHAPING & FILING TOOLKIT:
jeweler's file

sandpaper, 400 grit

BEADS & FINDINGS STASH:
blue pearl, 6mm, 1

blue pearls, 5mm, 3

champagne pearl, 2mm, 1

cushion crystal, 5mm, 1

silver bead cap, 6mm, 1

silver clasp (purchased), 1

topaz beads, 5mm, 1

FABRIC & SEWING STASH:
brown silk ribbon, ½" (13mm) wide, 6" (15cm) long

OTHER:
water

adhesive

bowl for dying

tea bag

vintage/antique book pages

Creating the Bird's Nest

1 Cut Wire
Cut 36" (91cm) of 24-gauge steel wire. Rub the wire with sandpaper to remove any coating.

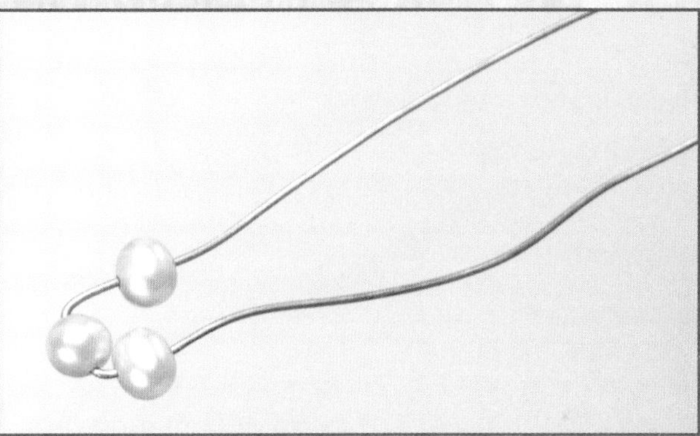

2 Add Pearls
Slide three 5mm pearls onto the wire.

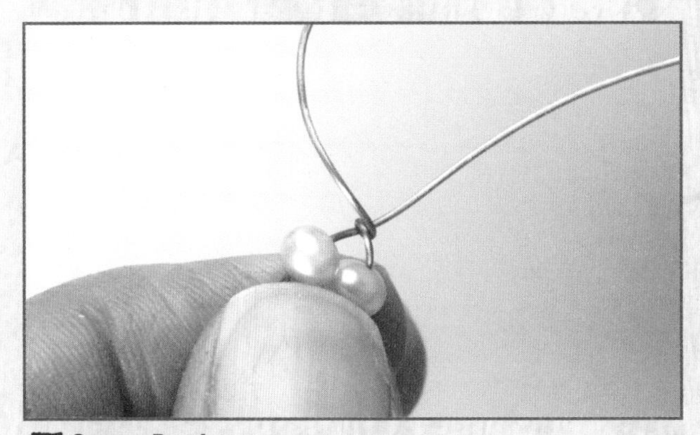

3 Secure Pearls
Bend the wire to form a triangle with the beads, then twist the wire to secure the pearls in place.

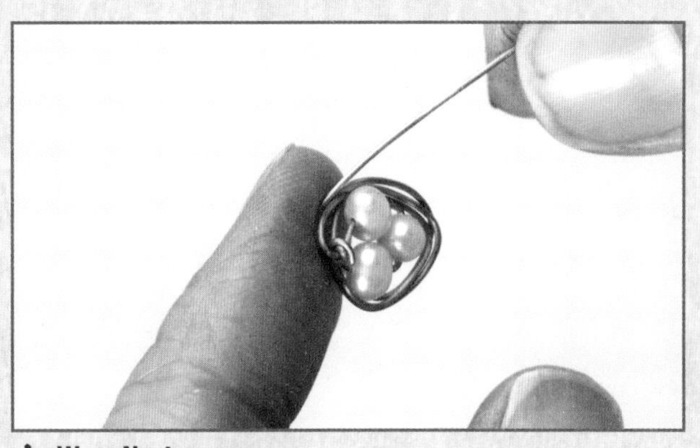

4 Wrap Nest
Wrap the wire around the pearls in a circular motion about eight times. Wrap one of the tails into the nest to secure.

5 Turn Loop on Nest

With the other wire tail, turn a loop (see page 15) using round-nose pliers. Wrap excess wire around the loop and trim.

6 Dye Lace

Boil 2 ounces (60ml) of water. Add one tea bag (we used Earl Grey) and let the tea steep for ten minutes. Place the lace into the tea and allow it to remain submerged until the desired color is achieved. Remove the lace from the tea and allow the lace to dry.

7 Cut and Drill Tubing

With a bench pin and a jeweler's saw fitted with a #2 blade, cut a ½" (13mm) piece of tubing. (See *Using a Jeweler's Saw*, page 19. For another example of cutting tubing, see page 69.)

With a drill fitted with a 1⁄16" drill bit, drill a hole through the center of the tube. You will use the tube as a bale.

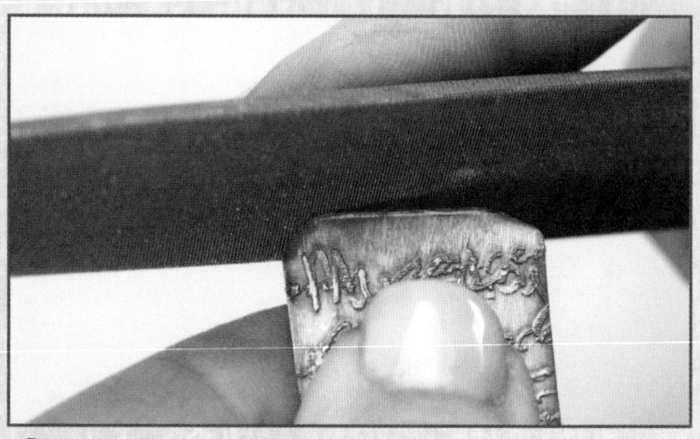

8 Cut Book Cover

Using metal shears, cut a piece of copper to measure ¾" × 1¼" (19mm × 32mm).

Snip and file the corners to round them and eliminate any rough or sharp edges.

9 Drill Holes in Book Cover

Locate the center of the longer side of the copper. Drill a hole using a drill fitted with a 1⁄16" drill bit in the center and near the edge. Drill a second hole on the opposite edge. File any sharp edges.

10 Drill Another Hole

Drill another hole, this time in the center near the edge of one of the shorter sides of the strip.

11 Fold Book Cover
With the copper piece positioned to hang over the edge of a bench block, create a fold at the center point of the metal.

12 Create Book Signature
Layer pages from vintage books with the dyed linen to create a signature of pages.

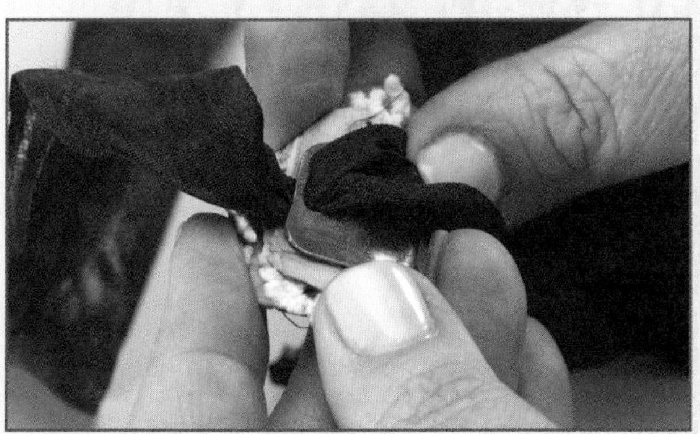

13 Combine Book Elements
Thread a piece of ribbon through the hole in the short end of the folded copper. Place the signature within the fold.

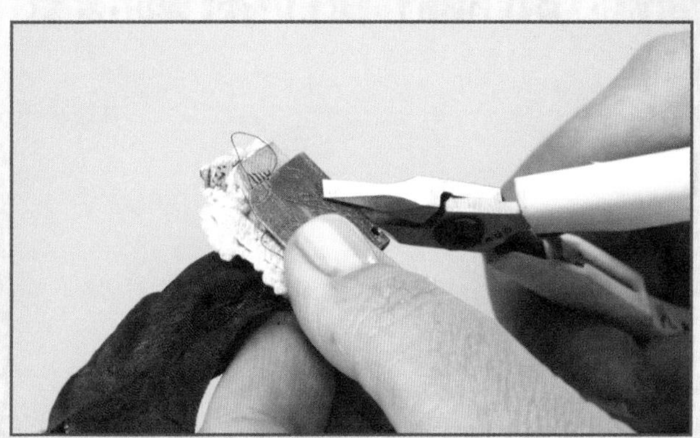

14 Pinch Book to Tighten
Secure the pages within the copper cover by pinching the cover with pliers if necessary.

15 Tie Book Closed
Wrap the ribbon around the book and tie it into a simple knot.

16 Add Nest to Ribbon

Slide the loop of the bird's nest charm onto one end of the ribbon. Tie a simple knot to secure the ribbon.

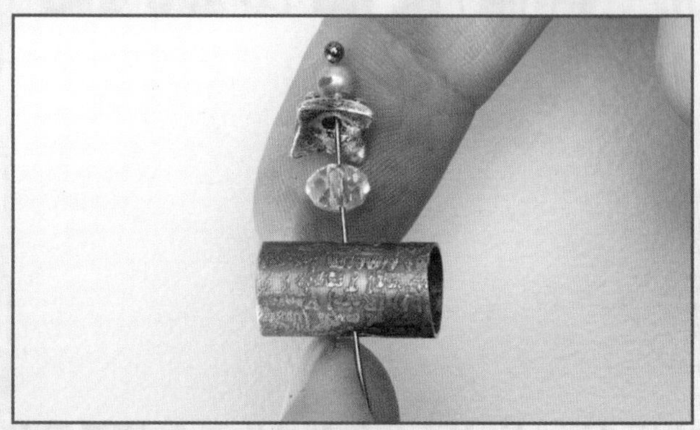

17 Add Beads to Tube Bale

Onto one headpin add: one 2mm champagne pearl, one 6mm silver bead cap and one 5mm cushion crystal. Slide the headpin through the holes drilled in the tube bale.

18 Secure Head Pin on Bale

Turn a loop on the other side of the bale and wrap wire to close the loop. Trim any excess wire.

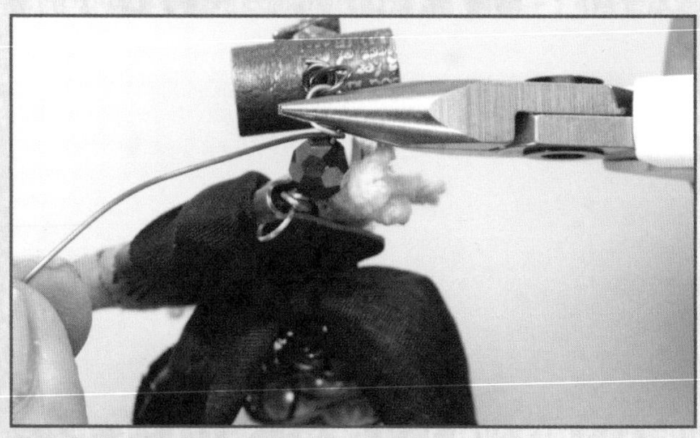

19 Attach Book to Bale

To join the book to the bale, cut a 3" (8cm) piece of 24-gauge gunmetal wire. Create a loop and place it through the hole drilled in the book. Wrap the wire to secure. Slide a 5mm topaz bead onto the wire, and turn a second loop at the top of the bead. Slide this loop through the loop on the bale and wrap the wire to close.

20 Assemble Chain

Open one 10mm jump ring and slide the purchased silver clasp onto it. Slide the open jump ring through the last link of the brass chain, then close the ring (see *Opening and Closing Jump Rings*, page 15). Slide the end of the chain without the clasp through the bale and out the other side.

21 Add Bead Dangle to Silver Chain

Slide one 6mm blue pearl onto a silver headpin. Using round-nose pliers, turn a loop above the pearl. Slide the loop through the last link of the silver chain. Wrap the wire around the loop to close.

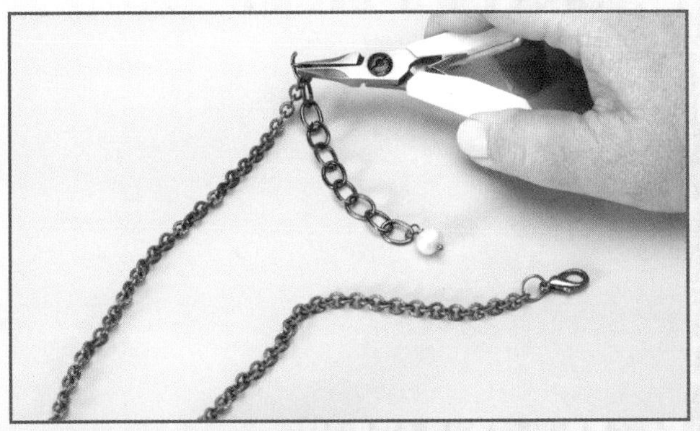

22 Attach Silver and Brass Chains

Open the end link of the silver chain and attach it to the end link of the brass chain. Close the link.

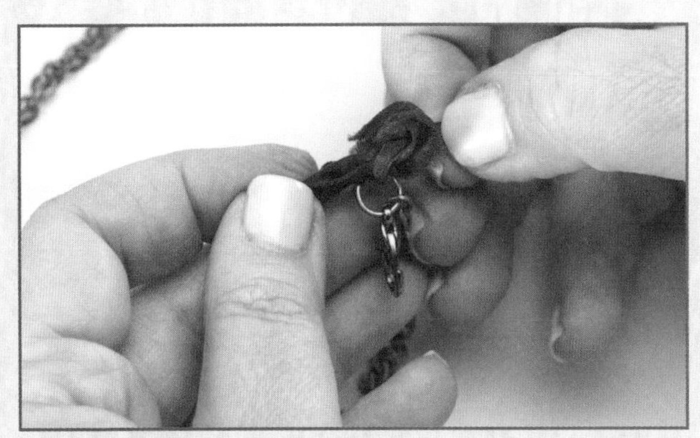

23 Embellish with Ribbon

Cut 2" (5cm) of brown silk ribbon and tie it to the jump ring at the base of the clasp.

FOREVER LOVE NECKLACE

Adding a dollop of resin to an open-back bezel is much like creating a little window to the soul when a favorite word or phrase is also added. Both of us are true romantics at heart, always rooting for the hero and heroine to come together at the end of the movie or book. That said, *Forever Love* is not only a nod to romantic sensibilities but also the kindness that lives in all of us—kindness that is pure when shared with others in a true sense.

WHAT YOU'LL NEED

METAL, ETCHED AND RESHAPED:
nickel silver, 24-gauge, 4" × 4" (10cm × 10cm)

OTHER METAL:
annealed steel wire, 24-gauge

silver headpins, 28

silver jump rings, 5mm, 3

silver jump rings, 10mm, 10

JEWELRY TOOLKIT:
ball-peen hammer

bench block or wood block

circle cutter

dapping block and dappers

flat-nose pliers

forming pliers

round-nose pliers

wire cutters

SAWING KIT:
jeweler's saw and #2 blade

SHAPING & FILING TOOLKIT:
jeweler's file

BEADS & FINDINGS STASH:
aquamarine cushion crystals, 4mm, 20

apatite cushion crystals, 8mm, 9

aquamarine cushion crystals, 10mm, 9

open-back bezel

FABRIC & SEWING STASH:
cream crushed velvet ribbon, ½" (13mm) wide

cream silk ribbon

scissors

sewing machine

taupe thread

DARKENING & PATINAS KIT:
microcrystalline wax

OTHER:
baby wipes

packing tape

printed transparency (cut to fit into bezel)

resin kit

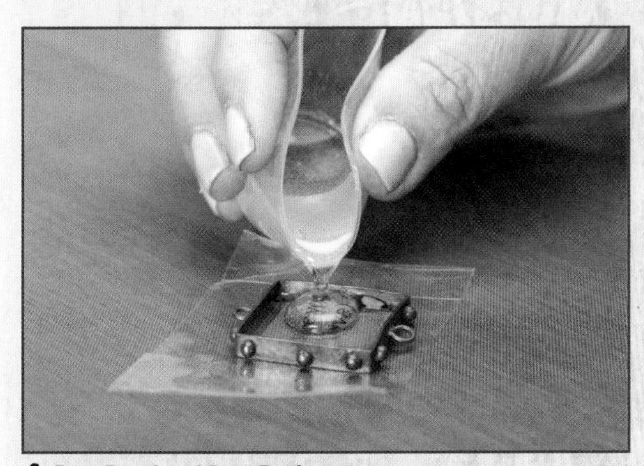

1 Prep Bezel and Pour Resin
Place a strip of packing tape onto the back of the bezel. Burnish all edges to ensure the tape is well adhered to the metal.

Mix the resin according to manufacturer's directions. Pour the resin into the bezel until the bezel is half full. Allow the resin to dry for three hours.

2 Place Transparency in Bezel
Lay the transparency on the partially dried resin.

3 **Add More Resin**
Mix more resin and pour it into the bezel, filling the bezel to the top edge. Allow the resin to dry for at least twenty-four hours.

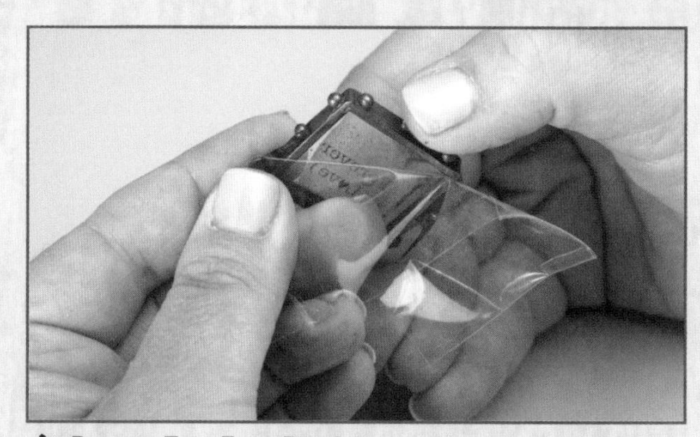

4 **Remove Tape From Bezel**
Once the resin has dried, remove the packing tape from the back of the bezel. Remove any sticky residue with a baby wipe if necessary.

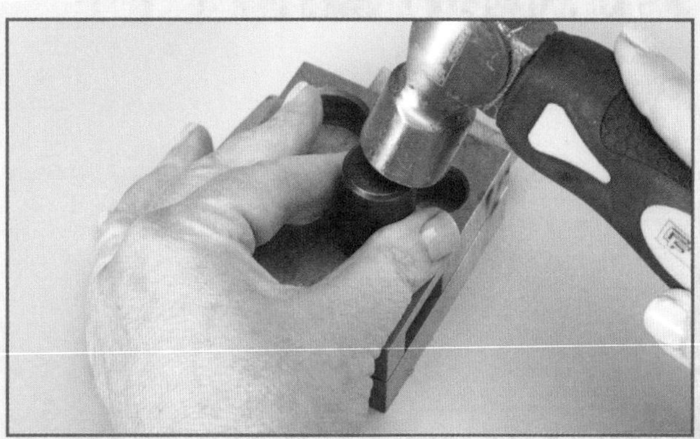

5 **Punch Discs**
Using a circle cutter and a ball-peen hammer, punch one ¾" (19mm) circle and one and ½" (13mm) circle from the nickel silver. (See *Using a Circle Cutter* on page 18.)

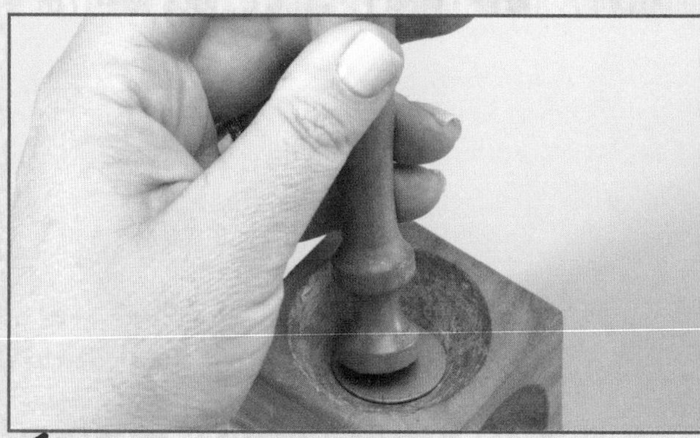

6 **Dome Smaller Disc**
Place the ½" (13mm) disc into the 1" (25mm) round of the dapping block and dome until the desired cupping is achieved. (See *Using a Dapping Block/Doming a Circle*, page 18, for instructions.)

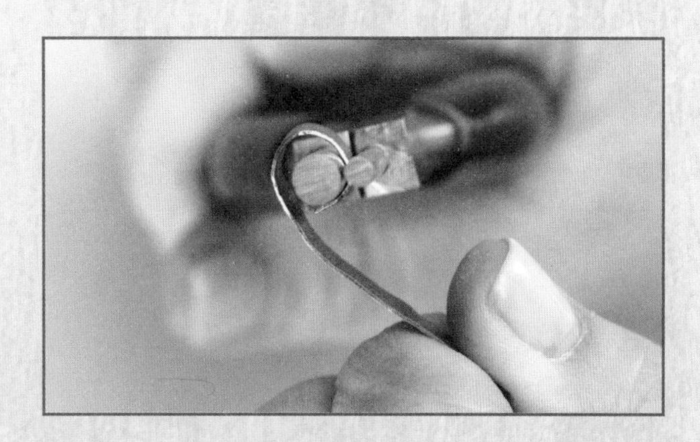

7 **Cut and Form Links**
Using a jeweler's saw fit with a #2 blade, cut seven strips, each measuring 2" × ¼" (5cm × 6mm) from the nickel silver. (See *Using a Jeweler's Saw*, page 19.)

Place one end of a nickel silver strip into the forming pliers. Using a rolling motion, roll the end of the metal to the center of the strip. Flip the strip over in your hand so the unrolled end is on top and repeat the rolling motion on this end and in the same direction to finish the link. Create seven links total. (See finished links from multiple angles in the main project photo, page 34.)

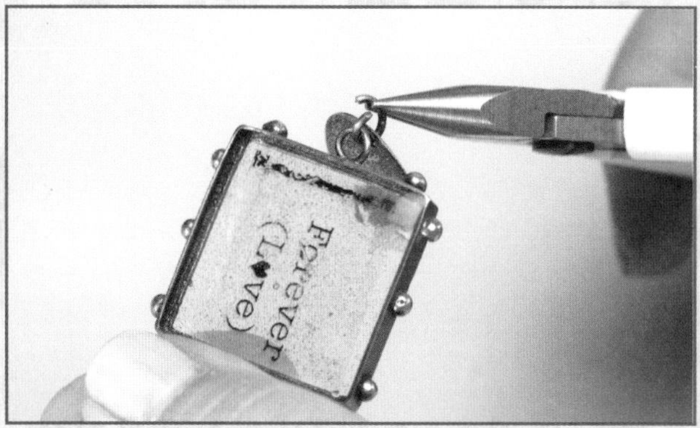

8 Drill Holes in Larger Disc

Using a drill fitted with a 1/16" drill bit, drill three holes in the large disc: two at the top and one at the bottom center. Each hole should be about 1/8" (3mm) from the edge of the disc.

9 Attach Large Disc to Bezel

Attach one 5mm nickel silver jump ring to the top bale of the bezel (see *Opening and Closing Jump Rings*, page 15). Add the larger jump disc to the open jump ring and slide the jump ring through the bottom drilled hole. Close the jump ring.

10 Create 10mm Crystal Links

Cut 4" (10cm) of 24-gauge annealed steel wire (use wire cutters). Using round-nose pliers, turn the wire to create a loop. Bring the wire tail around the loop and wrap it around. Trim excess wire. Place one 10mm aquamarine cushion crystal onto the wire. Turn the top wire to create a second loop, and bring the tail around the loop and wrap the loop closed. (See *Making a Wrapped Link*, page 16.)

Make two more of these links, joining all three to make a chain.

11 Create Beaded Chain

Slide one 4mm aquamarine cushion crystal onto each of six headpins. Turn a loop in each.

Slide one 8mm apatite cushion crystal onto each of three headpins. Turn a loop in each.

Attach two 4mm crystal loops and one 8mm crystal loop to one loop of each of the three 10mm crystal links.

Add a jump ring to the remaining free link of one of the 10mm crystal links.

12 Attach Chain to Disc

Slide the jump ring through one of the holes in the top of the disc.

13 Create Second Beaded Chain

Mimicking the directions in step 11, create a second chain:

Create a chain consisting of five 10mm aquamarine cushion crystal links.

Slide one 4mm aquamarine cushion crystal onto each of ten headpins. Turn a loop in each. Slide one 8mm apatite cushion crystal onto each of four headpins. Turn a loop in each.

Attach two 4mm crystal loops and one 8mm crystal loop to one loop of each of four of the 10mm crystal links.

Add the remaining two 4mm crystal loops to the last of the 10mm crystal links.

Add a jump ring to the remaining free link of one of the 10mm crystal links and attach the jump ring to the remaining hole in the disc.

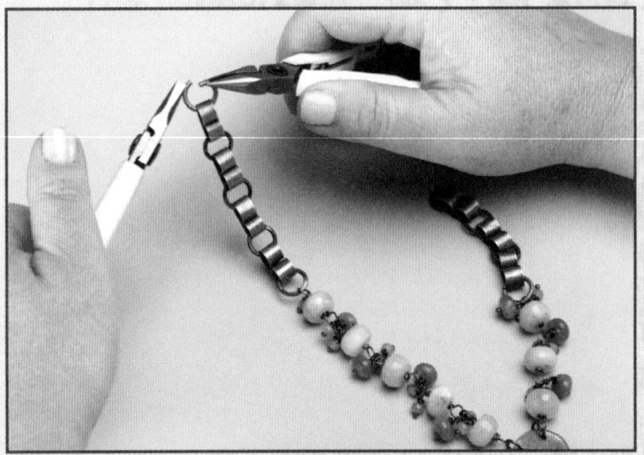

14 Make Metal Link Chain and Attach to Beaded Chain

Connect three of the nickel silver links (from step 7) with four jump rings in this order: jump ring/link/jump ring/link/jump ring/link/jump ring (leave the last jump ring open).

Attach this chain to the shorter of the beaded chains by sliding the open jump ring through the loop that holds the two 4mm crystal loops and one 8mm crystal loop. Close the jump ring.

Then connect four of the nickel silver links with five jump rings in this order: jump ring/link/jump ring/link/ jump ring/link/jump ring/ link/jump ring. Leave the jump rings on each end open.

Attach this chain to the longer of the two beaded chains, in the same manner as above. Close this jump ring. The jump ring on the loose end of the chain will remain open.

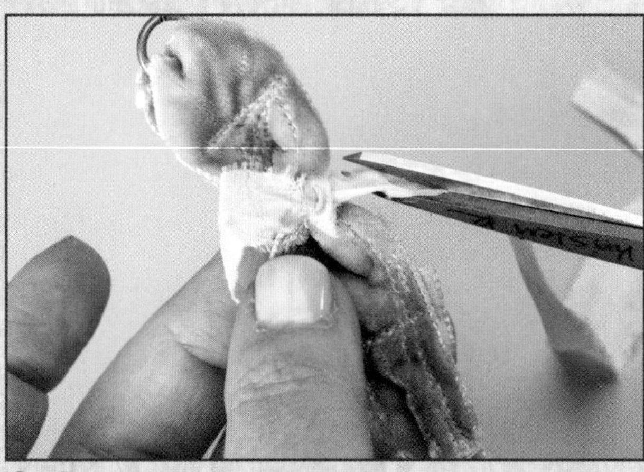

15 Creating Velvet Ribbon Link

Cut 8" (20cm) of cream-colored crushed velvet ribbon. Fold the ends of the ribbon into the center of the piece. Place the strip into a sewing machine and sew in a random manner to tack all ends down. Onto the velvet ribbon, tie two small strips of cream silk ribbon.

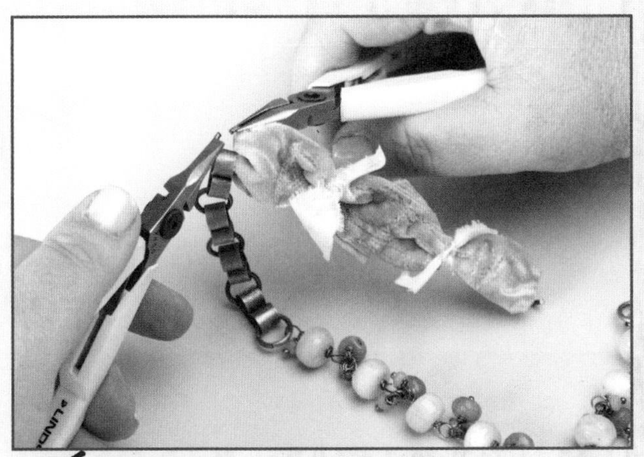

16 Attaching Velvet Link

Slide the velvet link onto the jump ring left open in step 15. Close the jump ring. Slide an open jump ring onto the other end of the velvet link.

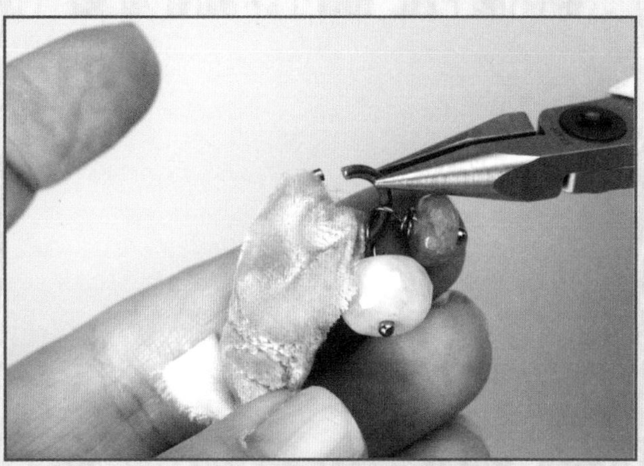

17 Create and Attach Wrapped Dangles

Make two wrapped dangles: one with an 8mm apatite cushion crystal and one with a 4mm aquamarine cushion crystal (see *Making a Wrapped Dangle*, page 16). Add the dangles to the open jump ring on the end of the velvet link. Leave the jump ring open.

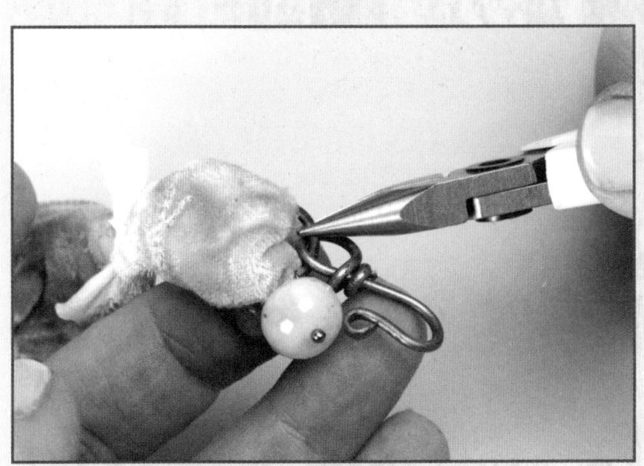

18 Make and Attach Hook Clasp

Create a hook clasp (see *Making a Hook/Clasp, page 17*). Add it to the open jump ring and close the jump ring.

19 Finish the Necklace

Create a dangle consisting of one 8mm apatite cushion bead and a domed disc. Attach this dangle to the closed loop on the bottom of the resin centerpiece.

Create three wrapped dangles: slide one 4mm aquamarine cushion crystal onto each of two headpins and one 8mm apatite cushion crystal onto another headpin. Open the jump ring that joins the resin centerpiece to the larger disc, slide on the dangles, and close the jump ring.

GRACE TO GROW NECKLACE

Grace to Grow is the perfect project for practicing your skill at cutting perfect curves and lovely angles. A sweet little bird speaks of grace and beauty in its simple nature, while wrapped eternity links come together to create a chain that is adorned with wonderful pearls and natural leather.

Finding elements that speak to you and then combining these elements is one of the best ways to identify your style and play a bit with an array of colors and textures. When creating the bird, think about not only words but markings that speak to you, as this project is the perfect personal statement.

You will find templates for *Grace to Grow* on page 122. You can also print them out directly from the *Making Etched Metal Jewelry* companion page. Visit CreateMixedMedia.com/MEMJ-companion.

WHAT YOU'LL NEED

METAL, ETCHED AND RESHAPED:
nickel silver, 24-gauge

OTHER METAL:
bronze headpins, 4

bronze wire, 18-gauge

bronze wire, 22-gauge

steel jump rings, 18-gauge, 5mm, 1

steel jump rings, 18-gauge, 8mm, 1

steel jump rings, 18-gauge, 10mm, 3

steel wire, 18-gauge

JEWELRY TOOLKIT:
ball-peen hammer

bench block

center punch tool

doming block and dapping set

flat-nose pliers

forming pliers

round-nose pliers

wire cutters

SHAPING & FILING TOOLKIT:
jeweler's file

sandpaper, 400 grit

sandpaper (2000A)

SAWING KIT:
drill and 1/16" drill bit

jeweler's saw and #2 blade or metal shears

rubber cement

DARKENING & PATINAS TOOLKIT:
darkening solution

Gilder's Paste

microcrystalline wax

soft cloth

BEADS & FINDINGS STASH:
milk white agate, 4mm, 1

potato pearls, 15mm, 4

white agate, 30mm, 1

FABRIC & SEWING STASH:
metallic thread, several spools

suede coring, 16" (41cm)

OTHER:
cardstock

scissors

1 Sawing the Nickel Silver
Adhere the template to the nickel silver with rubber cement. Using a jeweler's saw (see *Using a Jeweler's Saw*, page 19) or metal shears, cut out the bird shape. Remove the template from the metal and file any rough edges from the metal.

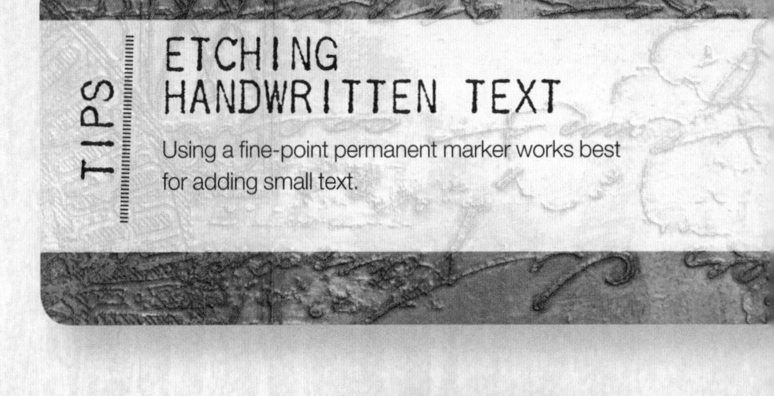

TIPS

ETCHING HANDWRITTEN TEXT

Using a fine-point permanent marker works best for adding small text.

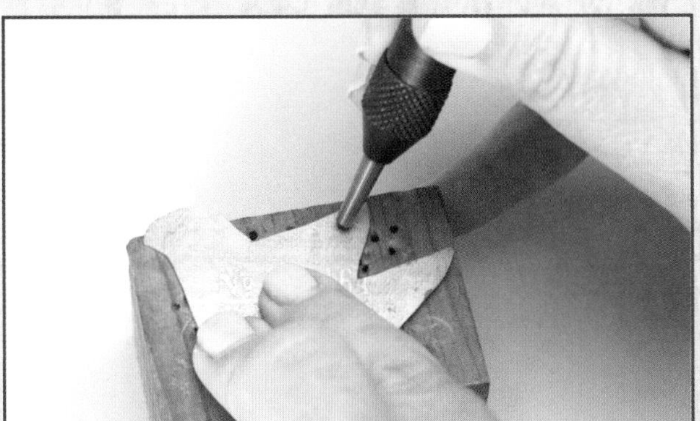

2 Create Guide Points
With a center punch tool, create a guide point at the tip of the bird's wing and near the bottom center of the bird.

3 Drill Holes
With a drill fitted with a 1/16" drill bit, drill holes at the marked locations.

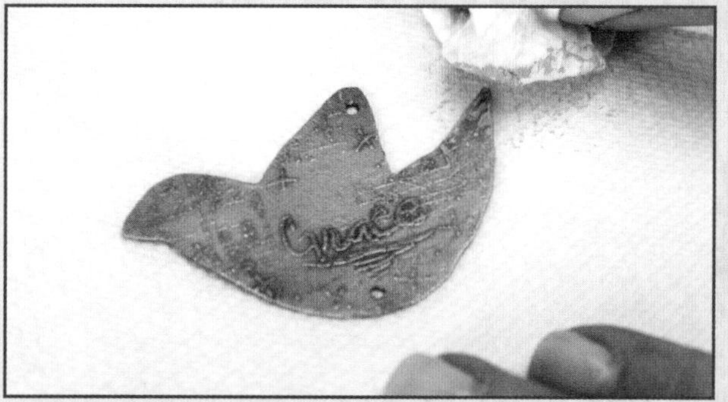

4 Add Patina

Add a patina to the bird using Gilder's Paste and microcrystalline wax. (See *Darkening and Adding Patinas*, page 20.)

5 Cut and Sand Wire

Cut 52" (132cm) of 18-gauge steel wire. Using 400-grit sandpaper, roughly sand the wire. Then cut the 52" (132cm) of wire into four 10" (25cm) pieces and one 12" (30cm) piece.

Cut four 8" (20cm), 22-gauge pieces of bronze wire. Sand wire with 400-grit sandpaper to a dull finish.

6 Hammer Wire

Using a ball-peen hammer and a bench block, hammer all nine pieces of wire In a random fashion, flattening some sections more than others. Flatten each end of each section of the wire.

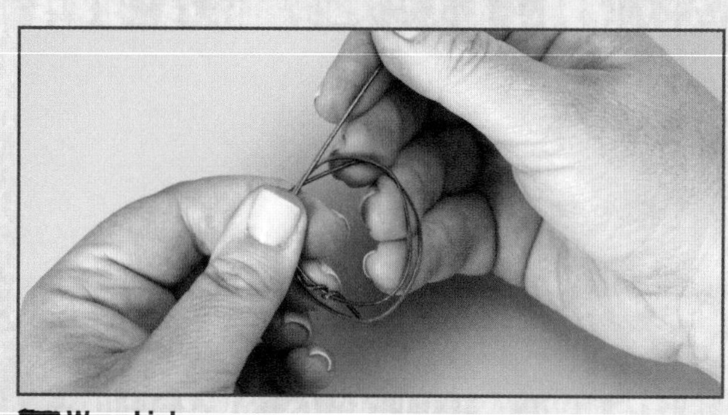

7 Wrap Links

Wrap a 10" (25cm) piece of steel wire into a circular shape consisting of two circles.

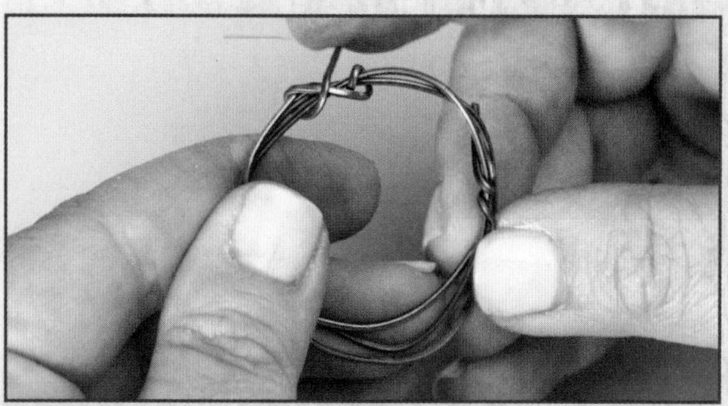

8 Close Link

Wrap one flattened end of the wire over the rounded link to close. Repeat with the remaining loose end to close the link.

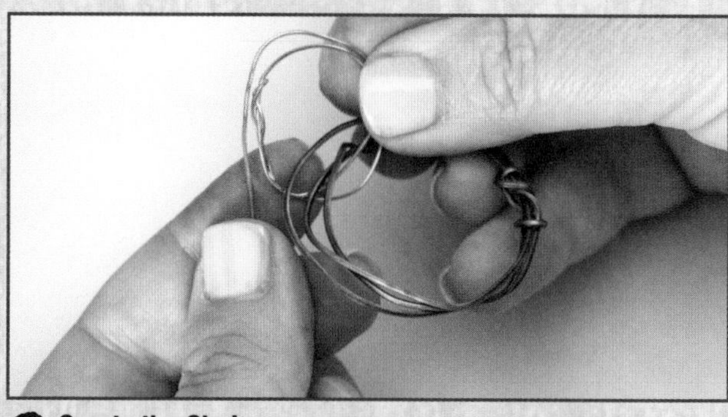

9 Create the Chain

Wrap an 8" (20cm) piece of bronze wire into a circular shape consisting of two circles. Slide this bronze link through the steel link created in step 8, and wrap the flattened ends to close the link.

10 Create and Add Next Link

Create another steel link as in steps 6–7, but pass it through the bronze link before you close it. Then add another bronze link and pass it through the last steel link before wrapping.

11 Create Link Chains

Repeat steps 7–10 so there are two chains, each consisting of four links.

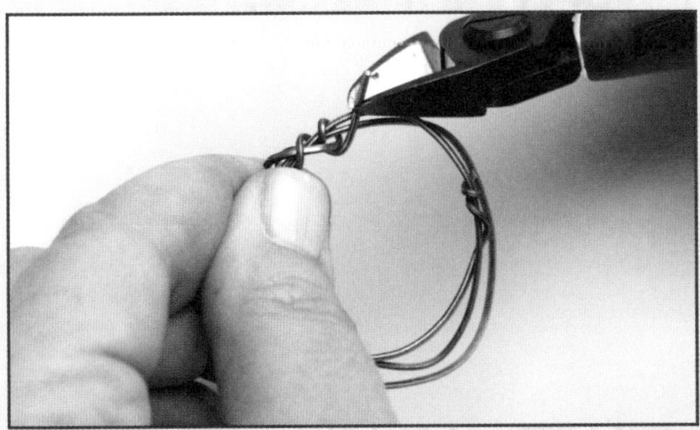

12 Add Large Link

Wrap a 12" (30cm) piece of steel wire into a circular shape consisting of three circles. Slide this link through the last bronze link created in each piece of chain, and wrap to close.

13 Create and Attach Bead Dangles

Place one 15mm potato pearl onto each of four bronze headpins. With round-nose pliers, create a loop above each pearl on each headpin. Place the loop through one steel link, then wrap the loop closed. Repeat with all pearl headpins, attaching one to each steel link in the chain. (See *Making a Wrapped Dangle*, page 16.)

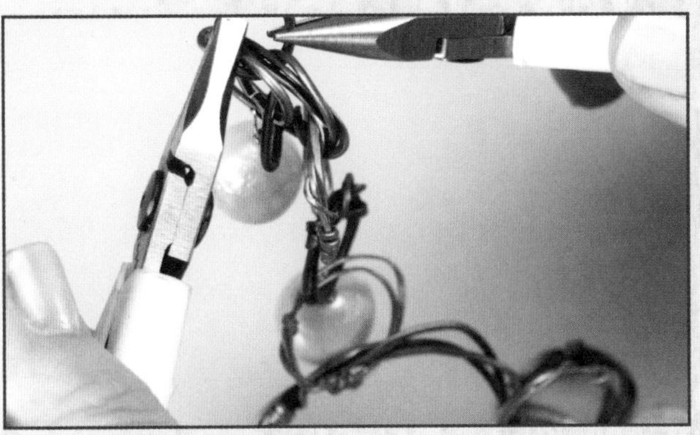

14 Attach Jump Rings

Open three 10mm steel jump rings and link them together (see *Opening and Closing Jump Rings*, page 15). Attaching the last jump ring to the ending steel link on one side of the chain

15 Add Suede Cording

Thread the suede cording through the end jump ring. Double the cording so it is doubled to a length of 8" (20cm).

Create a simple fold-over knot ¾" (19mm) from the jump ring.

16 Add Clasp and Close Cording

Make a clasp for the necklace (see *Making a Hook/ Clasp*, page 17). Run the two open ends of the cording through the loop on the clasp. Cut 12" (30cm) of 22-gauge bronze wire, and wrap it around the cording to secure the ends. Trim excess wire.

17 Secure Wire

Using flat-nose pliers, crimp the bronze wire tightly.

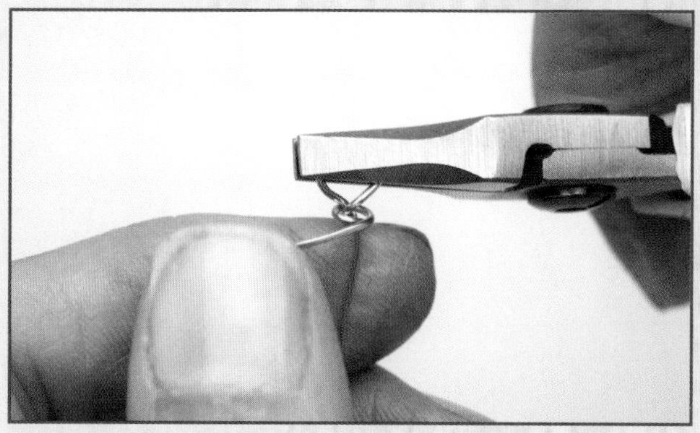

18 Create Agate Link

The white agate bead you are working with should measure about 1½" (4cm) from hole to hole. Cut 10" (25cm) of 18-gauge bronze wire. About 4" (10cm) from the end of the wire, create a loop with round-nose pliers. Wrap the wire and trim excess.

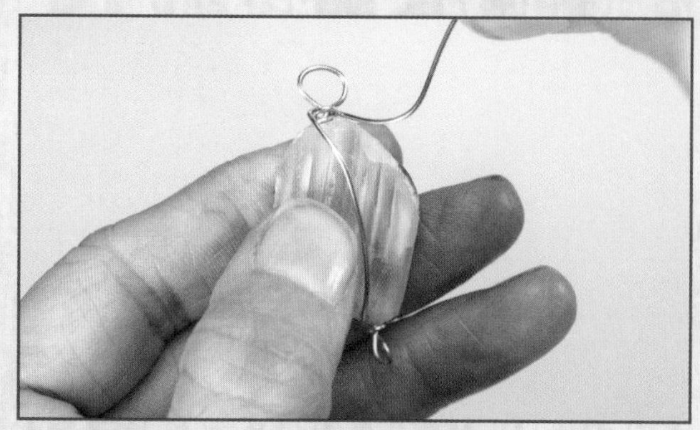

19 Wrap Stone With Wire

Place the agate bead onto the wire. Create a second loop on the other end of the bead using round-nose pliers. Wrap any excess wire over one flat surface of the bead and around the neck of the top loop. Then wrap the wire down the other side of the bead and around the bottom loop. Trim any excess wire.

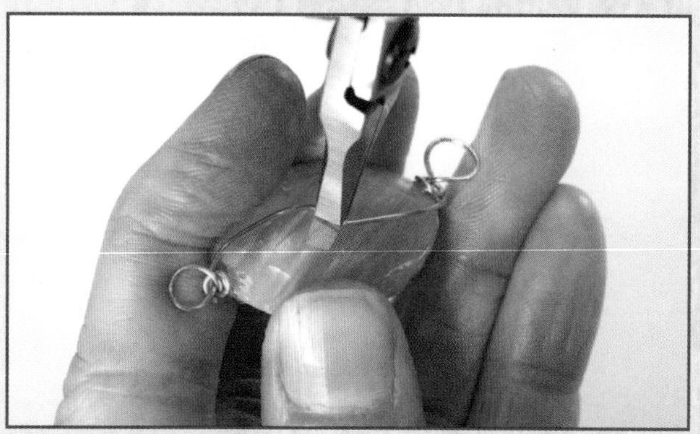

20 Embellish Wire

With flat-nose pliers, pinch the wire near the middle of bead and twist it to create a zigzag design. Repeat on the other side of the bead.

21 Create Tassel

Cut a piece of cardstock to measure 1½" × 3" (4cm × 8cm). Working off the spools of thread, wrap the thread around the 1½" (4cm) side of the card-stock until the desired thickness is achieved.

22 Secure Tassel

Secure the top of the tassel with a 5" (13cm) piece of thread tied in a square knot. Slide the tied thread off the cardstock.

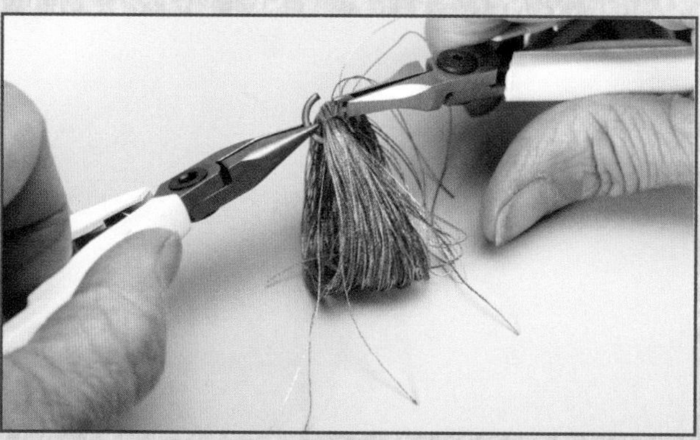

23 Add Jump Ring to Tassel

Open a 10mm jump ring and attach it to the tassel (see *Opening and Closing Jump Rings,* page 15).

24 Add Wire and Beads

Wrap a bit of 22-gauge bronze wire around the neck of the tassel where it meets the jump ring. Add a few 3mm bronze beads in a random fashion, leaving a 1" (25mm) tail in the wire. Wrap any excess wire through the wire wraps to camouflage, and trim if necessary.

25 Open Tassel

Use scissors to cut the bottom of the tassel open.

26 Join Agate Bead and Tassel

Open the jump ring that's attached to the tassel and slide it through the bottom loop in the agate link. Close the jump ring.

27 Join Bird Charm and Agate Link

Add a 5mm jump ring to the top link of the agate link. Slide on the bird charm (use the hole at the bottom of the charm), and close the jump ring.

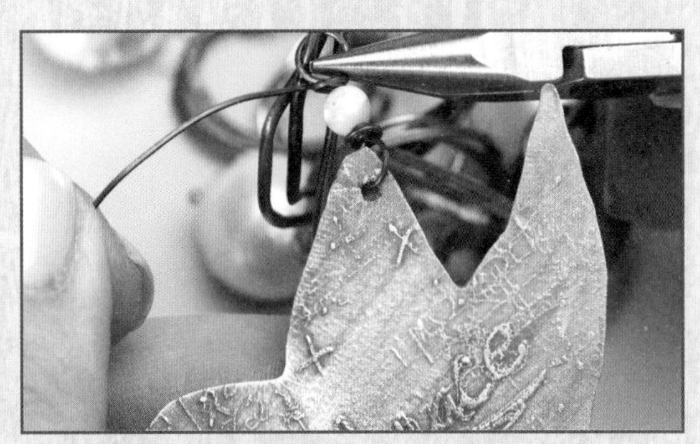

28 Create Link at Top of Bird Link

Create a wrapped loop link (see *Making a Wrapped Link*, page 16) and place it through the hole in the bird's wing. Wrap the link closed, and trim excess wire.

29 Add Smaller Agate Bead

Add a 4mm milk white agate bead above the loop created in step 28. Create a second loop above this bead, but before closing it, attach this loop through the base of the largest steel loop link. Wrap the wire and trim any excess.

FOREVER MORE CUFF & BAR BRACELET

This piece is a perfect example of how simplicity is as intriguing as its complex cousins.

By adding a layer of simple typewriter text, a background is provided to a favorite word and a story is written. The addition of lush velvet creates a wonderful cuff that feels delightful against the wrist. We promise that you will want to adorn yourself with this delightful cuff forever more.

You will find templates for *Forever More* on page 122. You can also print them out directly from the *Making Etched Metal Jewelry* companion page. Visit CreateMixedMedia.com/MEMJ-companion.

WHAT YOU'LL NEED

METAL, ETCHED AND RESHAPED:
nickel silver, 24-gauge, 2" × 2" (5cm × 5cm)

OTHER METAL:
brass headpin, 1

bronze wire, 24-gauge

silver chain, 10mm, 4" (10cm)

silver headpins, 2

silver wire, 22-gauge

JEWELRY TOOLKIT:
bracelet mandrel

flat-nose pliers

round-nose pliers

wire cutters

SHAPING & FILING TOOLKIT:
jeweler's file

rawhide mallet

SAWING KIT:
drill and 1⁄16" drill bit

jeweler's saw and # 2 blade

metal shears

wood block or bench pin

BEADS & FINDINGS STASH:
clasp, purchased

flat crystal, 15mm

gray potato pearl, 8mm

leaf charm, 25mm

pink coin pearl, 10mm

square faceted pink quartz, 10mm

FABRIC & SEWING STASH:
pink velvet

taupe thread

OTHER:
graphite pencil

sewing machine

spray sealant or microcrystalline wax

1 Saw Metal

Using a jeweler's saw, saw the nickel silver into two pieces: one to measure 1¼" × 2" (3cm × 5cm), and the other ½" × 1" (13mm × 25mm). (See *Using a Jeweler's Saw*, page 19.)

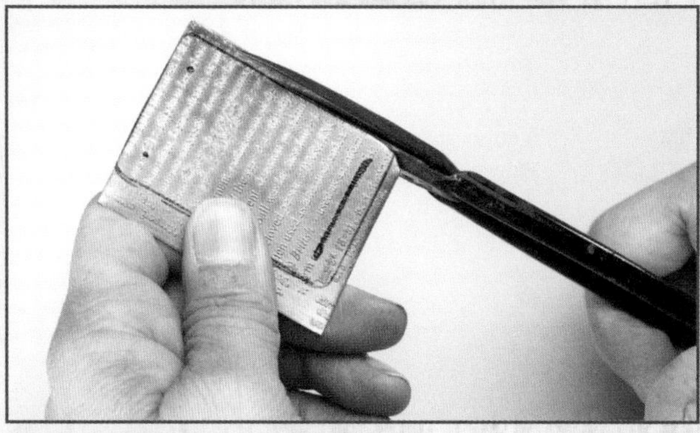

2 Trace Templates

Trace the large and small bar templates onto the metal, including fabric guides and markers for drilling holes. Use shears to cut these pieces.

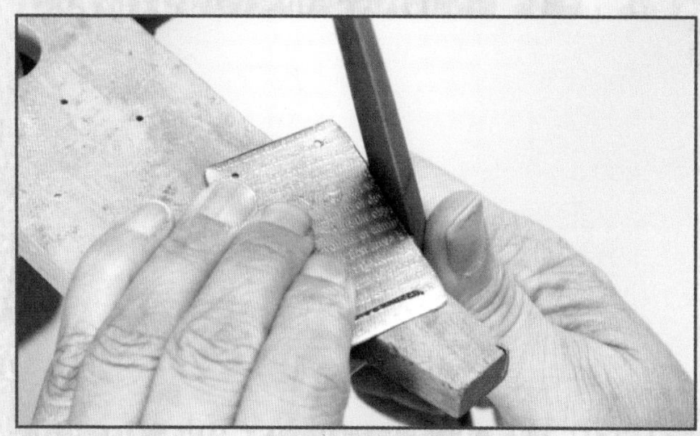

3 File Edges

File any rough edges on the metal pieces.

4 Drill Holes

Drill one hole on each side of the large bar using a drill fitted with a 1⁄16" drill bit. Drill one hole in the center of the smaller bar.

5 Drill Guides for Fabric Guide

Drill holes at each end of the traced fabric guide. This will allow you to insert the blade of the jeweler's saw and cut a guide from the center of the metal piece.

6 Insert Saw Blade
Insert the jeweler's #2 saw blade through one of the drilled holes, then reattach it to the saw frame.

TIPS

USING A JEWELER'S SAW

Add beeswax to your saw blade to ensure smooth sawing action. See *Using a Jeweler's Saw*, page 19, for more on using a jeweler's saw.

Or watch a video that reviews the entire process, step by step. Visit: CreateMixedMedia.com/MEMJ-companion.

7 Saw Out Fabric Guide
With the jeweler's saw, create an opening that measures ⅛" × 1" (3mm × 25mm), following the traced template lines. Repeat steps 4–7 to cut out the fabric guide on the smaller piece.

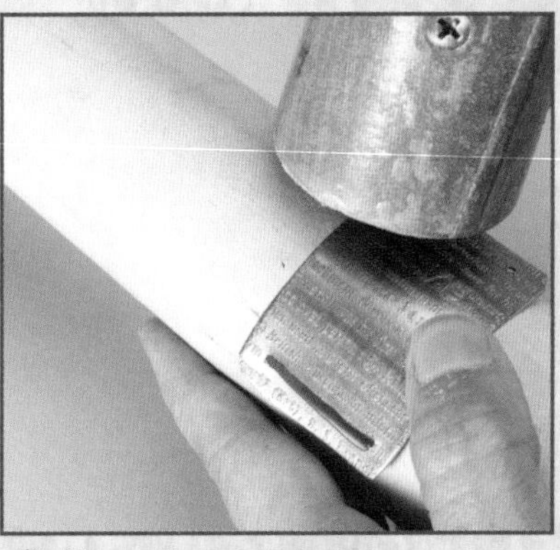

8 Shape Larger Metal Piece
Place the larger metal piece on a bracelet mandrel and use a rawhide mallet to shape it in such a way that it mirrors the curve at top of your wrist.

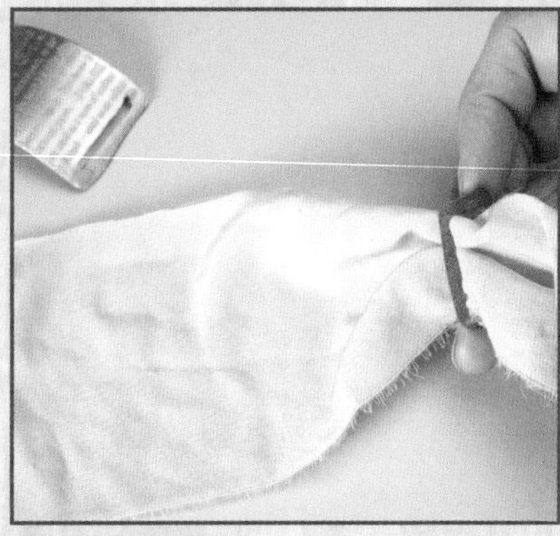

9 Prep Velvet
Cut 10" (25cm) of pink velvet and fold it in half. Slide the smaller bar into the center of the velvet and fold the fabric.

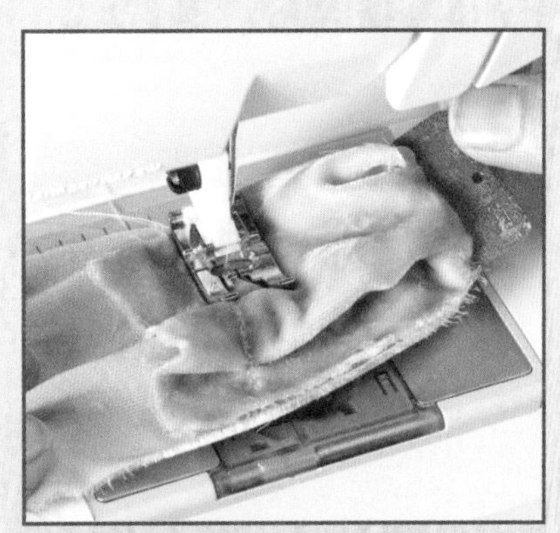

10 Sew Velvet
Using a sewing machine and taupe thread, embellish the fabric with a random pattern using a straight stitch. Be sure to tack the fabric down onto itself.

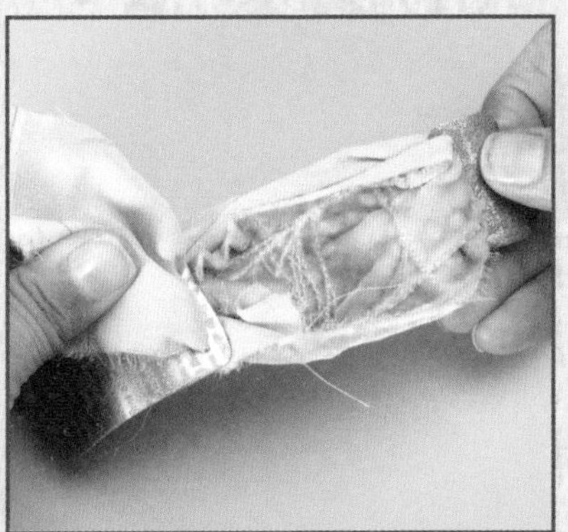

11 Adding Large Bar
Place the selvage end of the velvet through the guide of the larger bar, allowing 1½" (4cm) of the fabric to fold onto itself.

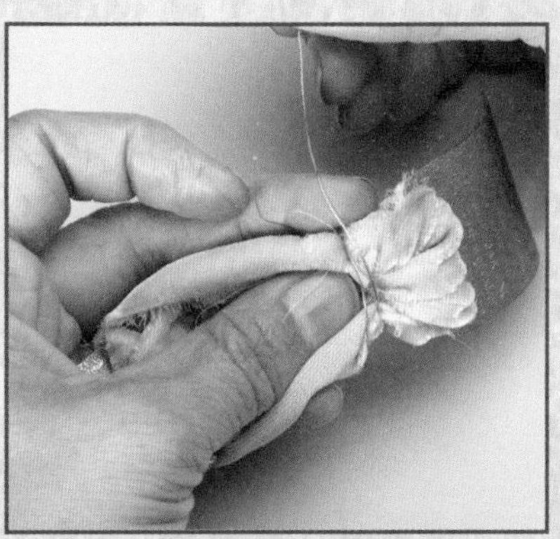

12 Preparing the Wire Wrap
Cut 18" (46cm) of 24-gauge bronze wire and wrap it around the fabric once.

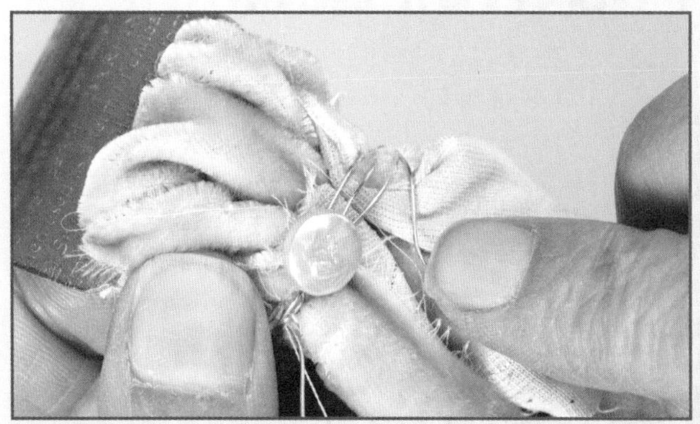

13 **Add Coin Pearl**

Thread a pink coin pearl onto the wire and center it on the top center of the pink velvet fold. Pull both ends of the wire around the fabric three times.

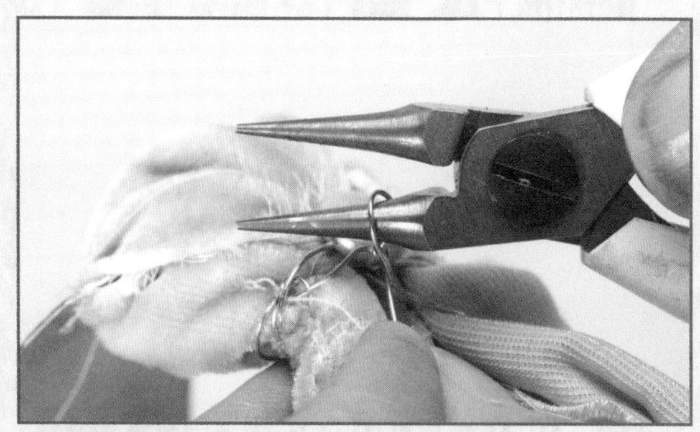

14 **Creating a Loop**

With round-nose pliers, create a loop 3" (8cm) from end of wire. Wrap the excess wire from both ends around the loop and tuck.

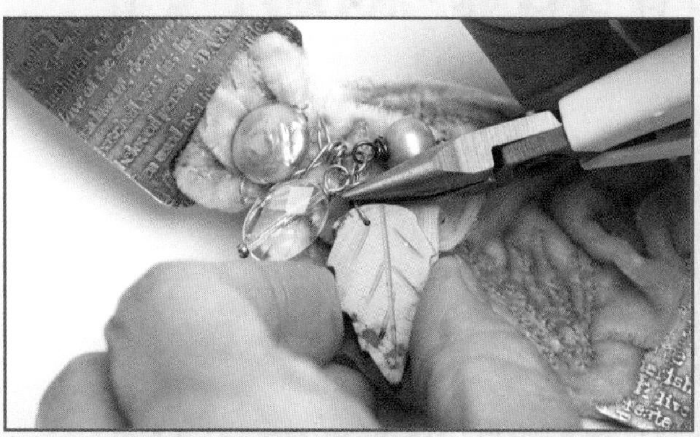

15 **Create and Attach Dangles**

Onto one brass headpin, add a flat crystal. Onto one silver headpin, add a gray pearl.

Create a loop in each headpin, just above the crystal and the pearl. Attach the loops to the loop created in step 14. Wrap the loops to close.

Cut a 6" (15cm) piece of 22-gauge silver wire. Create a loop 2" (5cm) from the end of the wire and place the loop through the drilled hole of leaf. Wrap the loop to close it. With the other end of the wire, create a loop at the top of the leaf. Attach this loop to the bronze wire loop as you did with the headpins. Wrap the wire to close.

16 **Attach Chain and clasp**

To one of the drilled holes on the larger bar, attach 1" (25mm) of purchased silver chain. Open the link on the other end of the chain and attach it to the other drilled hole.

Open the center link of chain and attach the purchased clasp. Close the link.

17 **Attach Pink Quartz Strand**

To the small bar, attach 3" (8cm) of silver chain through the drilled hole. Close the chain link. Onto one silver headpin, place the 10mm square faceted pink quartz. At the end of the headpin wire, create a loop using round-nose pliers. Place the loop through the last link of the chain, and wrap the loop to close it.

Add a depth of shading to the etched metal bars by rubbing graphite over them. Seal with a spray sealant or microcrystalline wax.

BILLOWING "S" LINKS BRACELET

When Ruth came up for the idea for this bracelet, neither of us had any idea how much we would like the outcome. While creating a sheet metal clasp, Ruth had one of those wonderful lightbulb moments that always reinvigorates us.

Perfectly divine links that look much like billowing curves are nicely linked and adorned with custom charms and pearls. I especially enjoy the large loops that attach the green crystals, as they help define the change in texture and color. The metal tab charms create a second palette for detail and imagery—one that is just delightful.

You will find templates for *Billowing "S" Links* on page 122. You can also print them out directly from the *Making Etched Metal Jewelry* companion page. Visit CreateMixedMedia.com/MEMJ-companion.

WHAT YOU'LL NEED

METAL, ETCHED AND RESHAPED:
nickel silver, 22-gauge, 4" × 4" (10cm × 10cm)

OTHER METAL:
jump rings, 10mm, 7

silver headpins, 4

JEWELRY TOOLKIT:
ball-peen hammer

bench block

circle cutter

doming block and dapping set

flat-nose pliers

forming pliers

rawhide mallet

round-nose pliers

wire cutters

SAWING KIT:
drill and 1/16" bit

metal shears

wood block

SHAPING AND FILING TOOLKIT:
jeweler's file

sandpaper,

BEADS AND FINDINGS STASH:
green faceted crystals, 5mm, 4

pearls, 4mm, 3

TIPS

USING SCRAPS OF METAL

This is a great project for using up leftover bits of etched sheet metal—the links look wonderful when they are composed of different textures and imagery.

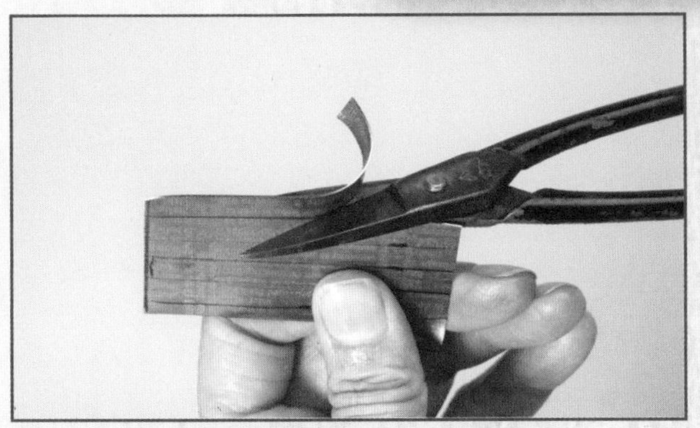

1 Cut Metal for Links and Clasp
Using shears, cut the nickel silver into strips measuring ¼" × 2½" (6mm × 6cm). Cut a total of seven strips.

2 Strengthen Metal
With a rawhide mallet and bench block, hammer each strip of nickel silver. Sand any rough edges.

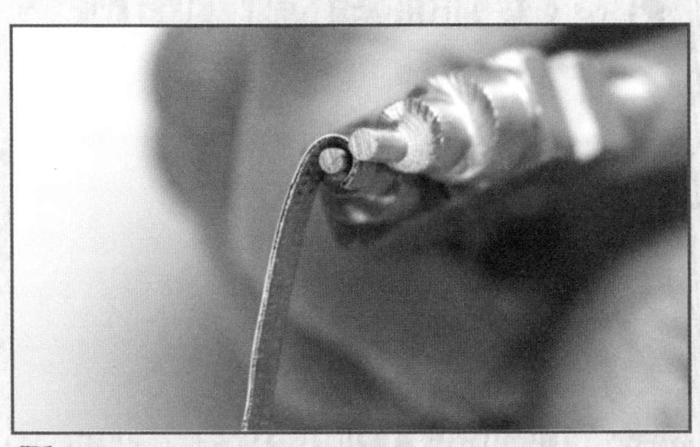

3 Form Link
Using 4mm forming pliers, roll one end until it touches the flat part of the strip.

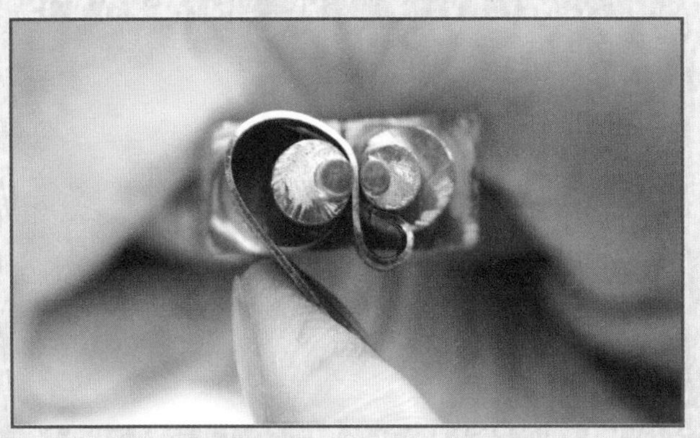

4 Continue Forming Link
Place the 5mm side of the forming pliers behind and just at the base of the first curve. Roll the strip in the opposite direction from the first curve.

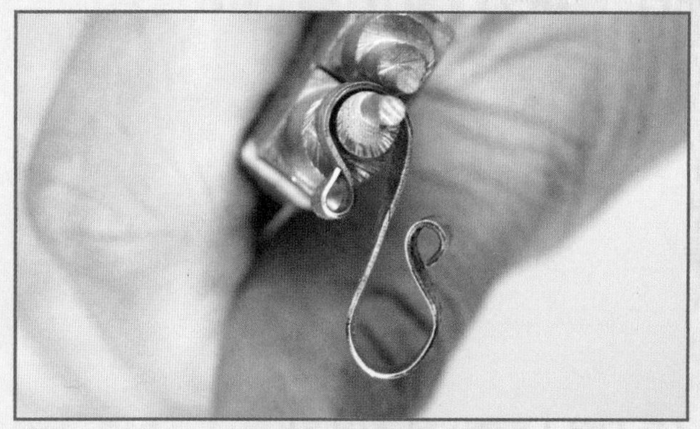

5 Finish Link

Repeat steps 3–4 on the other end of the strip to complete the link.

Make six more links following steps 3–5, for a total of seven links.

6 Join Links

Attach all seven links with 10mm jump rings, creating a chain. One end link will have a jump ring attached and one won't. You can use your fingers or flat-nose pliers and a light touch to squeeze the link closed and secure the jump ring within the curve.

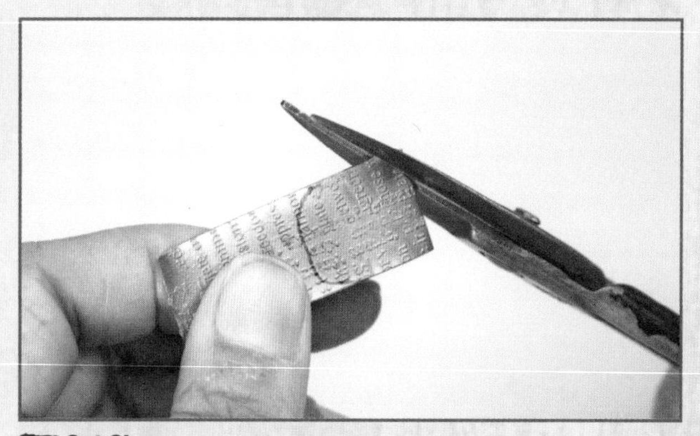

7 Cut Charms

Trace the charm template onto the nickel silver three times. Cut out all three charms.

8 Drill Charms

Using a drill fitted with a 1/16" bit, drill a hole near the center top of each charm.

9 Cut Circle for Clasp

Using a circle cutter, cut a 1" (25mm) circle (see *Using a Circle Cutter*, page 18).

10 Trace Center Cutout

Using a ½" (13mm) circle cutter as a template, trace an off-center circle ¼" (6mm) from the top of the cut circle. Draw an *X* in the circle so it will be easy to see.

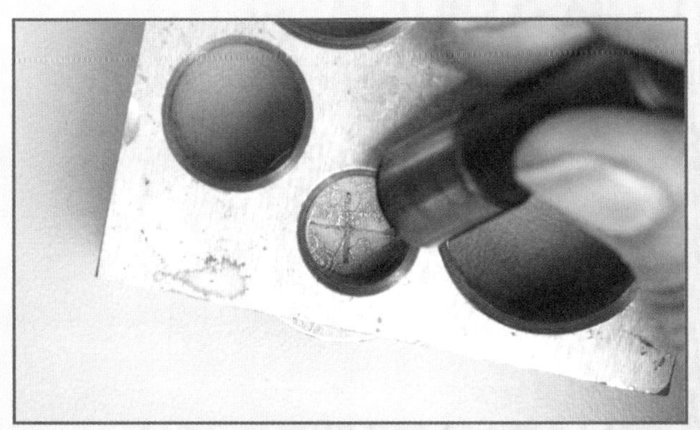

11 Cut Out Center of Clasp

Place the circle back into the cutter, lining up the traced circle with the ½" (6mm) guide. Punch out the circle.

12 Drill the Disc

Using a drill fitted with a 1⁄16" drill bit, drill a hole at top of the wide part of the circle.

13 Dome the Circle

Place the circle into the 1⅜" (35mm) round of a dapping block. Dome the circle (see *Using a Dapping Block/ Doming a Circle*, page 18).

Attach the clasp to one end of the bracelet by sliding the jump ring in the last link (step 6) through the drilled hole in the circle. You can use your fingers or the flat-nose pliers and a light touch to squeeze the link closed and secure the jump ring within the curve.

14 Create Bead Dangles

Slide one green crystal onto each of the four silver headpins. Using round-nose pliers, create a loop at the top of one of the crystals, and attach the loop to the first jump ring on left side of chain. Wrap the wire and trim any excess. Repeat this process with the remaining three crystal headpins, attaching them to the third, fifth and seventh jump rings.

Slide one pearl onto each of three headpins. Using round-nose pliers, create a loop at the top of one of the pearls, and wrap the wire to close the loop. Open a jump ring, and slide on one of the nickel silver charms and a pearl dangle. Attach the jump ring to the second jump ring in the bracelet. Close the jump ring. Repeat this process with the remaining two pearl headpins and charms, and attach the charms to the fourth and sixth jump rings.

TIPS

BRACELET LENGTH

The bracelet can be lengthened by adding additional jump rings and *S* links.

2 CONTINUING THE ETCHING JOURNEY

Now that you have experienced firsthand the many amazing ways etching can be incorporated into jewelry, it is time to take your journey a step further. In this chapter, we delve into projects that are a bit more advanced yet easily accomplished when following along step by step.

From a necklace that offers charm and a bit of bling to a bracelet composed of links, Chapter 2 gives you plenty of reasons to carve out as much creative time as possible. While the tools we use in Chapter 1 carry over to this portion of your etching journey, it is time to add to our toolkits. Here we introduce not only the torch but also the sewing machine.

Gather your supplies, and be sure to have your saw and bench pin at the ready, as there is no doubt that you will want to get as busy as you can as quickly as you can to create your own versions of these projects.

BE TRUE NECKLACE

Ruth, being who she is, sought a way to pay homage to my stamp line by creating a beautiful piece of jewelry for me to wear. Of course I was ecstatic to say the least, as I adore anything she creates.

What started out as a pendant adorning a lovely hand-crafted chain morphed into a project we chose to share with you here. This is perhaps one of our favorite projects—it truly marries both our styles and our creative sensibilities. Wrapped ribbon and a wire-wrapped clasp represent the collaboration of two dear and true friends.

You will find templates for *Be True* on page 123. You can also print them out directly from the *Making Etched Metal Jewelry* Companion page. Visit CreateMixedMedia.com/MEMJ-companion.

WHAT YOU'LL NEED

METAL, ETCHED AND RESHAPED:
brass, 24-gauge, 2" × 2" (5cm × 5cm)

OTHER METAL:
annealed steel wire, 19-gauge

bronze headpins, 3

bronze wire, 24-gauge

gunmetal wire, 22-gauge

gunmetal wire, 24-gauge

JEWELRY TOOLKIT:
forming pliers

round-nose pliers

wire cutters

SAWING KIT:
drill and 1/16" bit

metal shears

wood block

SHAPING & FILING TOOLKIT:
jeweler's file

BEADS & FINDINGS STASH:

faceted cream beads, 8mm, 4

gold pearls, 3mm, 2

oval topaz beads, 15mm, 3

pearl, 2mm, 1

round rhinestone trim, 4mm

smoky topaz beads, 3mm, 2

vintage pin or brooch

FABRIC & SEWING STASH:
cream raw silk ribbon, 6" (15cm)

gold sari silk, 24" (61cm)

taupe silk ribbon, 6" (15cm)

DARKENING & PATINAS KIT:
darkening solution

soft cloth

steel wool

OTHER:
jeweler's glue

jump ring

permanent marker

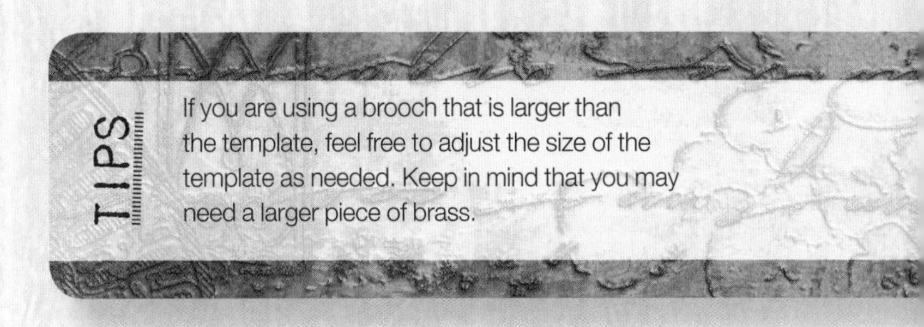

TIPS

If you are using a brooch that is larger than the template, feel free to adjust the size of the template as needed. Keep in mind that you may need a larger piece of brass.

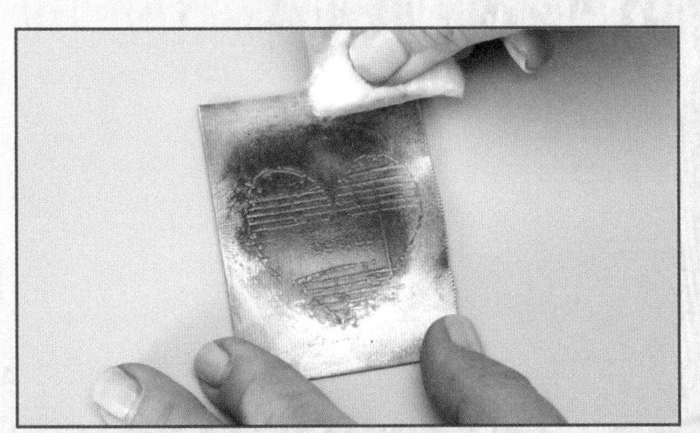

1 Darken Metal
Apply darkening solution to the brass with a cotton ball (see *Darkening and Adding Patinas*, page 20). Rinse it under running water, and dry it with soft cloth.

2 Buff Metal
With a piece of steel wool, clean the metal once more as this will buff it and remove any excess darkening solution residue.

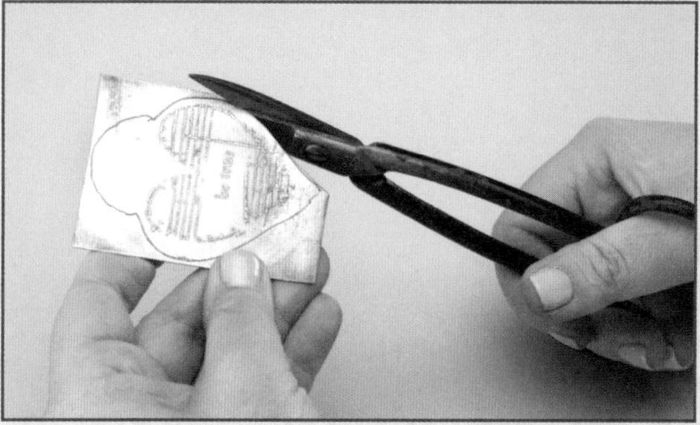

3 **Cut Out Heart Shape**
Trace the heart template onto the brass. Using shears, cut out the heart. File any sharp edges using a jeweler's file. Keep in mind that the extra space at the top of the template is where the brooch will attach to the chain.

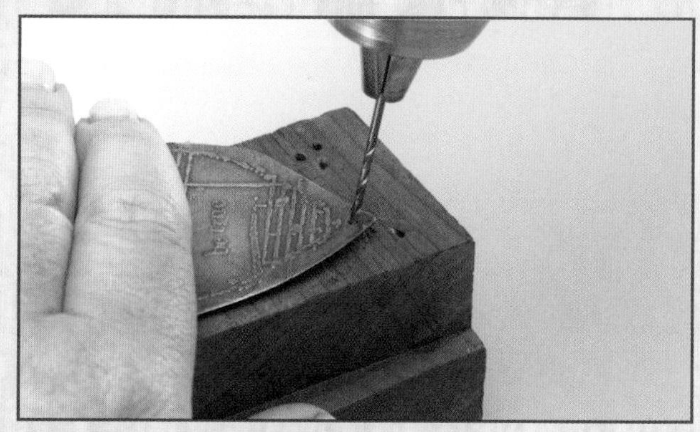

4 **Drill Hole at Point of Heart**
With a drill fitted with a 1⁄16" drill bit, drill one hole at the bottom point of the heart.

5 **Set Brooch and Rhinestone Trim**
Place the rhinestone brooch or pin at the top of the heart. Place a small drop of jeweler's glue onto the back of the brooch and adhere it at the top of the heart.

Using jeweler's glue, adhere rhinestone trim to the perimeter of the heart. Allow the glue to dry for an hour.

6 **Drill Guides**
In this case rhinestones were missing from the brooch and the resulting spaces were used as guide points. With a permanent marker, mark places where the holes should be drilled—these are the holes through which the chain will be attached. Drill the holes.

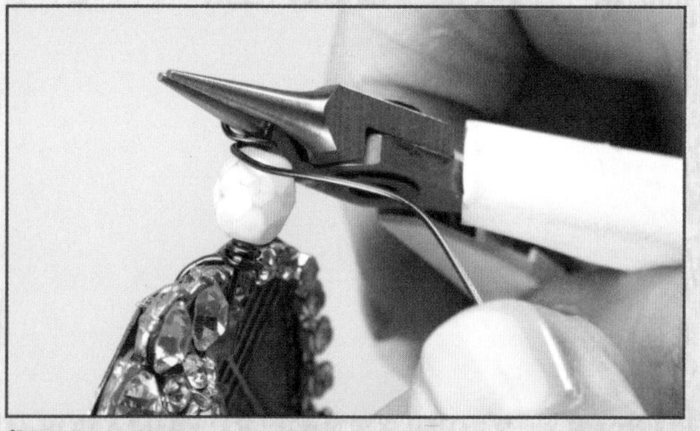

7 **Create Chain**
Using round-nose pliers, turn a loop in the 22-gauge gunmetal wire. Bring the tail through one of the holes at the top of the heart (through the brooch) and wrap the tail to close the loop. Trim excess wire. Add one 8mm faceted cream bead to the wire. Create a second loop, wrap the tail around the base, and trim any excess wire.

8 **Add Second Link to Chain**
With 22-gauge gunmetal wire, create another loop, this time threading the wire through the loop of the previous link before wrapping it. Onto this wire, add one 15mm oval topaz bead. Create a second loop, wrap and close it.

9 Continue Adding to Chain

Continue in this manner until you have a chain consisting of two faceted beads and two topaz beads.

10 Add Chain to Other Side of Centerpiece

As you did in steps 7–9, build a chain consisting of two 8mm faceted beads and one 15mm topaz bead. Leave the last link of the chain open for now.

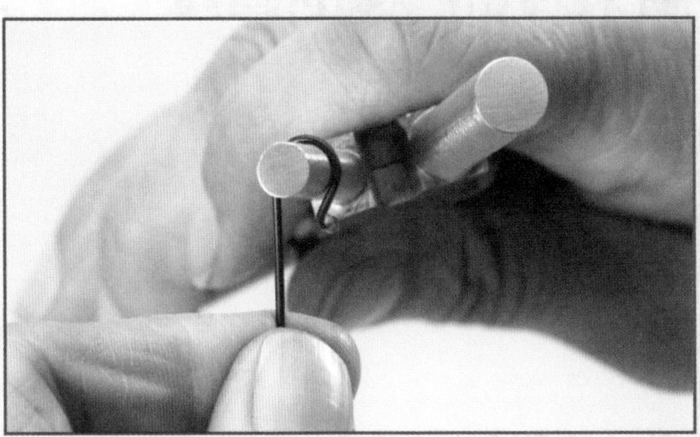

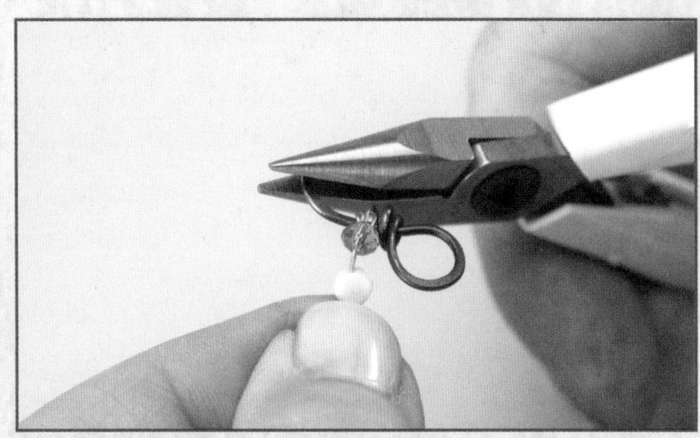

11 Create a Hook/Clasp

Sand a piece of 19-gauge steel wire to remove any manufacturer-applied coating and to give it a bit of an antiqued look. Use the wire to make a hook/clasp (see *Making a Hook/Clasp*, page 17).

12 Adding Wire and Beads to Clasp

Cut 3" (3cm) of 24-gauge bronze wire. Wrap the clasp with the bronze wire, starting near the bottom wrap. After six wraps, slide one 3mm smoky topaz crystal and one 2mm pearl onto the wire. Continue wrapping the wire until about three-quarters of the clasp has been covered.

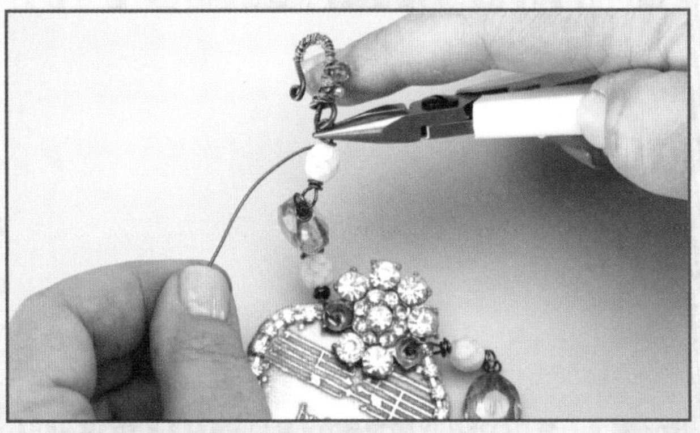

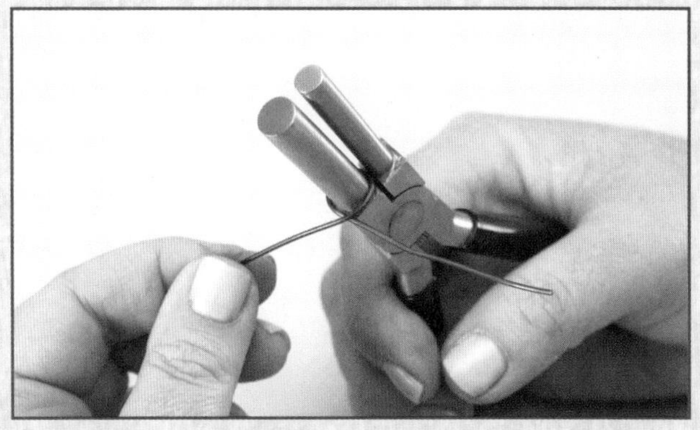

13 Join Chain and Clasp

Place the loop of the clasp onto the last link of the chain (see step 10). Wrap the loop to close.

14 Create Eternity Ring

Cut a 4" (10cm) piece of 19-gauge steel wire that has been sanded. At the halfway mark, wrap the wire to create a loop. (Forming pliers work well for this; a dowel would also work.)

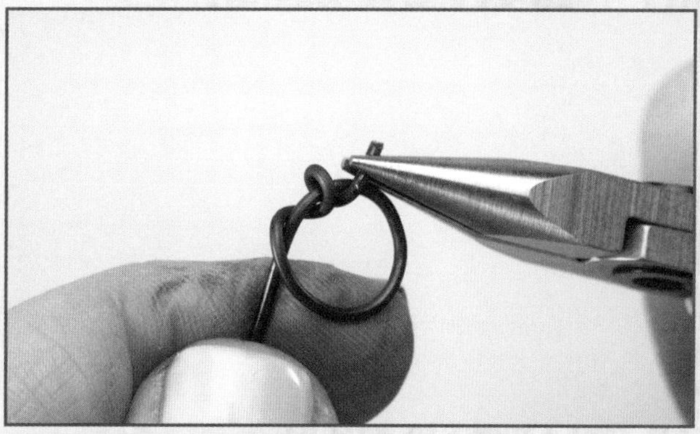

15 Wrap Excess Wire

Wrap the wire from one side of the ring around and through the loop. Trim excess wire from both sides of the ring.

16 Attaching Sari Silk

Slide the eternity ring onto a 24" (61cm) piece of sari silk. Fold the silk in half and allow the ring to slip to the center of the ribbon.

17 Securing Sari Silk

Fold 2" (5cm) of the silk onto itself to make a closed loop of the ribbon. Fold the overlapped ribbon, as shown. Cut 24" (61cm) of 24-gauge gunmetal wire. Wrap the wire around the fold until all wire has been used.

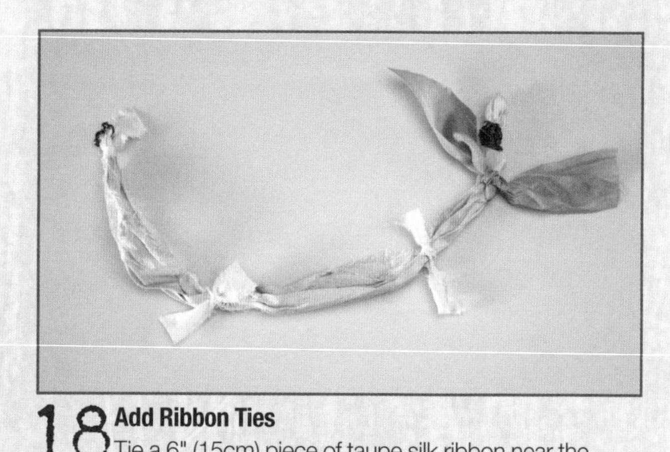

18 Add Ribbon Ties

Tie a 6" (15cm) piece of taupe silk ribbon near the wrapped wire.

Cut three 2" (5cm) pieces of silk ribbon and tie them on the sari silk, one every 3" (8cm) or so.

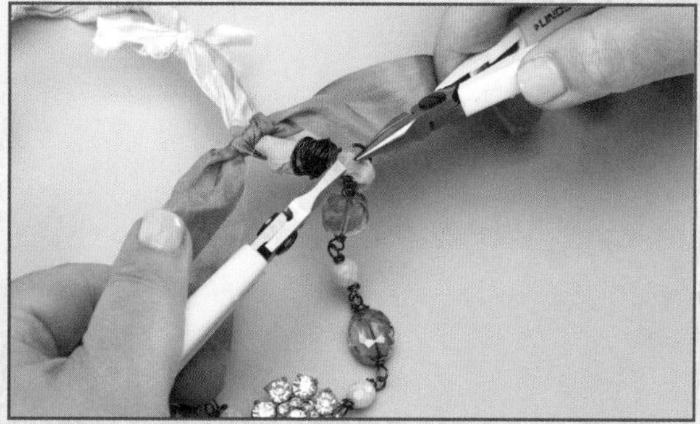

19 Add Jump Ring

Slide a jump ring through the wired end of the ribbon and the last loop on the longer chain, then close the jump ring.

20 Embellish with Bead Dangles

Make three bead dangles: Slide one 2mm gold pearl onto one headpin, one 3mm smoky topaz crystal onto another headpin and one 2mm gold pearl a third headpin. Create a loop in each headpin just above the bead, using round-nose pliers.

21 Attach Bead Dangles

Place the loop through the drilled hole near the bottom of the heart. Wrap any remaining wire around the base of each loop and trim the excess. (See *Making a Wrapped Dangle*, page 16.)

IN HER GARDEN RING

It is funny how we all have specific themes and objects we find ourselves attracted to—and how we seem to create around those ideas almost exclusively, sometimes for a considerable period of time. Ruth and I found ourselves drawn to oversize rings. It goes without saying that an oversize ring is a statement piece and that more often than not such a ring is not quite ... sensible. Fortunately, we all have those occasions when sensibility is easily thrown out the window and a statement piece is just perfect.

Creating a piece like this requires a few different processes. However, such processes are applicable to many other projects. Creating this ring thus becomes an entry point for a plethora of creative ideas. Enjoy as you hammer, pour, wrap and dome your way through the following pages.

You will find templates for *In Her Garden* on page 122. You can also print them out directly from the *Making Etched Metal Jewelry* Companion page. Visit CreateMixedMedia.com/MEMJ-companion.

WHAT YOU'LL NEED

METAL, ETCHED AND RESHAPED:
brass, 22-gauge, 2" × 2" (5cm ×5cm)

nickel silver, 24-gauge, 1" × 1" (25mm × 25mm)

nickel silver, 24-gauge, 4" × 1" (10cm × 25mm)

OTHER METAL:
brass screw and nut

JEWELRY TOOLKIT:
bench block

ball-peen hammer

doming block and dapping set

forming pliers

rawhide hammer

ring mandrel

SHAPING & FILING TOOLKIT:
jeweler's file

sandpaper (2000A)

SAWING KIT:
center punch

circle cutter

drill and 1⁄16" bit

jeweler's saw and #2 blade

metal shears

rubber cement

DARKENING & PATINAS TOOLKIT:
darkening solution

soft cloth

OTHER:
bowl filled with rice

E6000 or other strong adhesive

ledger paper

printed text

resin kit

1 Trace and Cut the Flower
Adhere the template to the brass with rubber cement. With a jeweler's saw or metal shears, cut the flower shape from the metal (see *Using a Jeweler's Saw*, page 19). Remove the template. File any rough edges.

2 Creating Disc
Using the 1" × 1" (25mm × 25mm) piece of nickel silver and a circle cutter, punch one ⅝" (15mm) circle (see *Using a Circle Cutter*, page 18).

3 **Dome the Disc**
Starting with the largest and deepest round on the doming block and the largest dapper, begin to dome the circle. As the dome forms, move it to smaller rounds within the block until the desired dome has been achieved (see *Using a Dapping Block/Doming a Circle*, page 18).

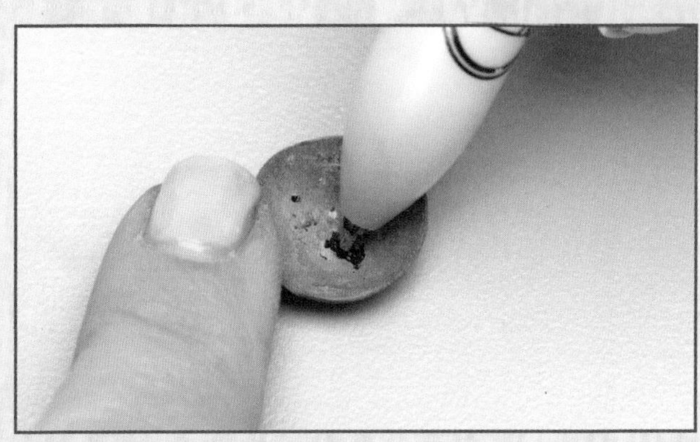

4 **Mark Center of Domed Disc**
Mark the center of the domed disc with a permanent marker and then with a center punch. Then, with the center punch, mark the center of the flower.

5 **Dome the Flower Shape**
Starting with the largest round on the doming block and the largest dapper, begin to dome the flower shape. As the dome forms, move it to smaller rounds within the block until the desired dome has been achieved.

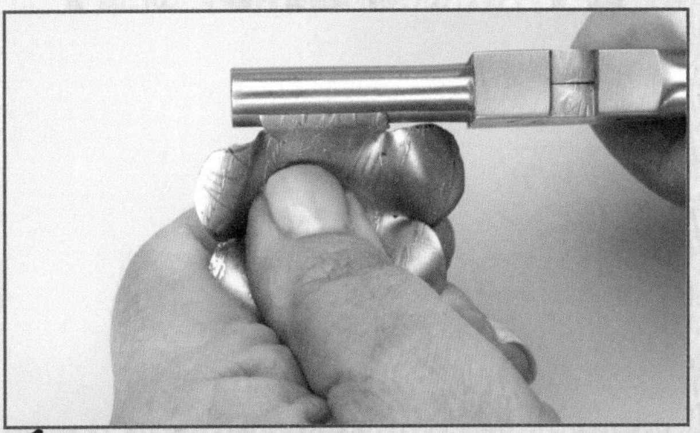

6 **Shaping Flower Petals**
Using forming pliers, shape the petals as desired. Once you've shaped the petals, you can re-dome the flower, if necessary, to achieve the shape you desire.

7 **Drill Through Center of Flower**
Drill a hole through the center of the flower.

8 Drill Through the Domed Circle

Using the center mark you punched in step 4, drill a hole in the center of the domed disc.

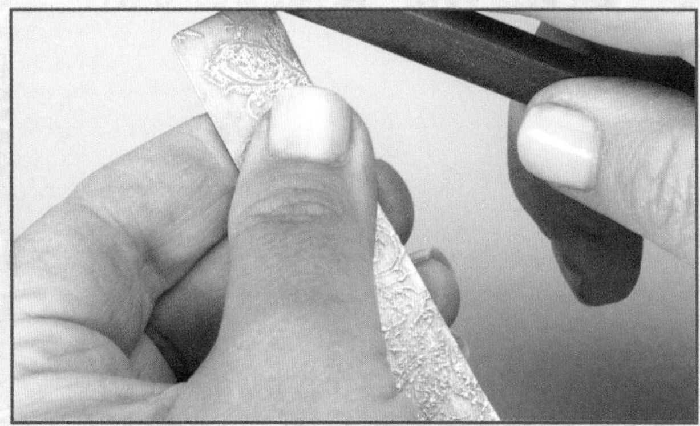

9 Cut and Shape Nickel Silver Ring Band

Cut the 24-gauge nickel silver into a strip measuring 3½" × ¾" (9cm × 19mm) using a jeweler's saw or metal shears.

Using metal shears, cut a curve at each corner of the ring band. If need be, file any sharp edges, using a jeweler's file.

10 Mark Guide for Drilling

With a permanent marker, make a drill guide in the center of the band.

11 Drill Center Hole

With a drill fitted with a 1/16" drill bit, drill a hole through the band.

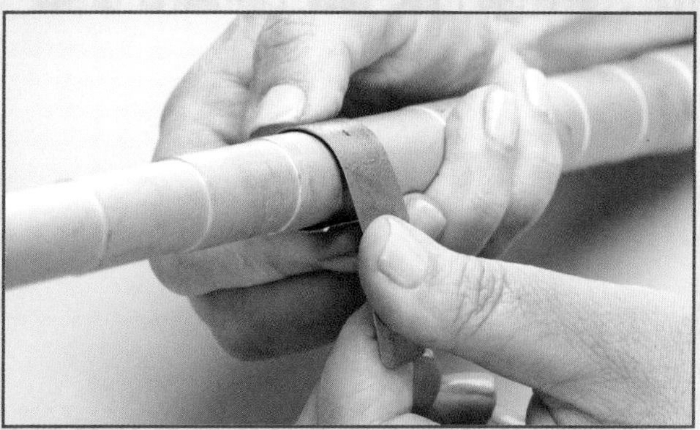

12 Shape Band Into Adjustable Ring

Place the metal strip onto the ring mandrel. Starting one size larger than your desired size, shape the band around the mandrel.

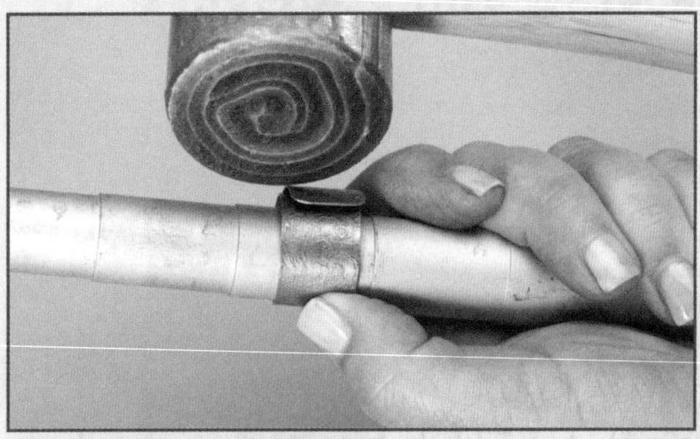

13 Hammer Band and Finish Sizing

Begin tapping on the band with a rawhide hammer, gradually forming the band around the mandrel.

Move the band down to the desired size on the mandrel and continue shaping it until the band is completely round.

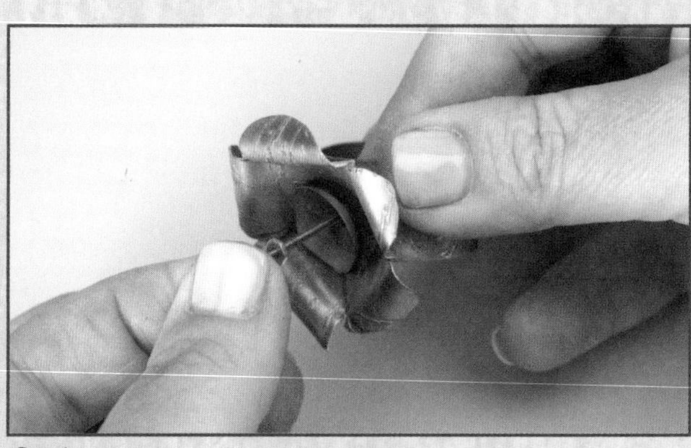

14 Join Flower and Ring Band

Place a screw through the ring band, then through both the flower and the domed disc. Secure the screw in place with a nut. Tighten the nut.

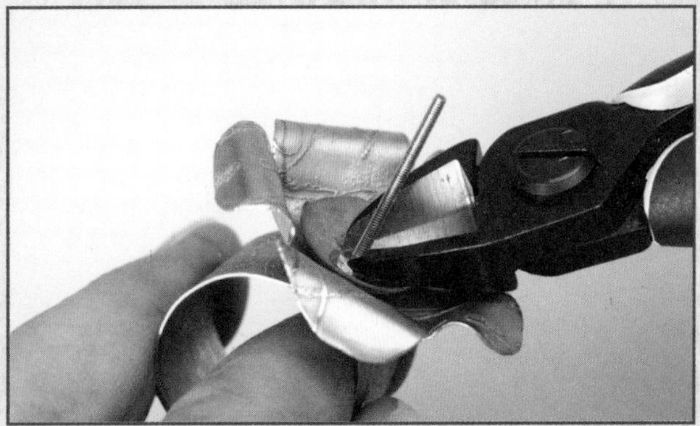

15 Trim Screw

Using wire cutters, trim the screw as close to the nut as possible.

16 Place Ring Into Bowl Filled With Rice

Place the ring into a bowl filled with rice to keep it level and steady. Glue a bit of text onto ledger paper and then place the ledger paper into the domed disc, covering the nut.

17 Mix Resin
Mix the resin according to manufacturer's directions.

18 Pour Resin
Fill the domed disc with resin and the allow resin to dry as per the manufacturer's directions.

TIPS

APPLY PATINA

Apply a patina to various areas of the ring if desired. Rub off any excess patina with soft cloth (see *Darkening and Patinas*, page 20).

MIST OF THE MOUNTAINS BRACELET

Ruth and I both have a history in Hawaii—we both resided there as children during the same time period. This experience created a memory within us that only Hawaii can create. Perhaps it is best to say this project is our simple ode to the shimmering mist that caresses the Hawaiian mountains, a mist that we have experienced in no other land.

Here we share our ideas for creating custom chain, a technique that is perhaps one of the most freeing and creative ways we can communicate our style through jewelry. When looking at brass tubing, one might not immediately envision it interconnected with handmade links and pearls. But this piece is unique and personal and that's what finding your own style is all about.

WHAT YOU'LL NEED

METAL, ETCHED AND RESHAPED:
brass, 22-gauge

brass tubing, ¼" (6mm) thick

copper, 24-gauge

nickel silver, 22-gauge

OTHER METAL:
annealed steel wire, 18-gauge

brass headpins, 15

silver jump rings, 5mm, 3

steel wire, 18-gauge

JEWELRY TOOLKIT:
ball-peen hammer

bench block

doming block and dapping set

forming pliers

round-nose pliers

wire cutters

SHAPING & FILING TOOLKIT:
jeweler's file

SAWING KIT:
bench pin

circle cutter

drill and $\frac{1}{16}$" bit

jeweler's saw and #2 blade, or metal shears

BEADS & FINDINGS STASH:
gold beads, 10mm, 6

gray iridescent pearls, 8mm, 6

silver bead caps, 2mm, 15

FABRIC & SEWING STASH:
gray silk ribbon

ruler

Sharpie marker

1 Measure and Mark Tubing
Using a ruler and a Sharpie marker, measure out eleven ¼" (6mm) marks on the etched tubing.

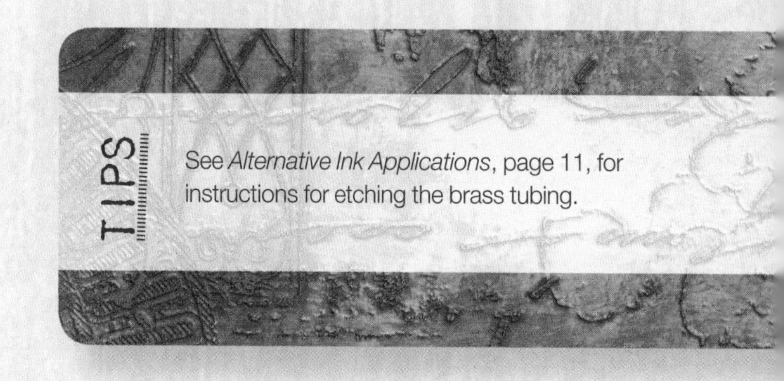

TIPS

See *Alternative Ink Applications*, page 11, for instructions for etching the brass tubing.

2 Cut Tubing
Using a jeweler's saw (see *Using a Jeweler's Saw*, page 19), cut the tubing along the marks.

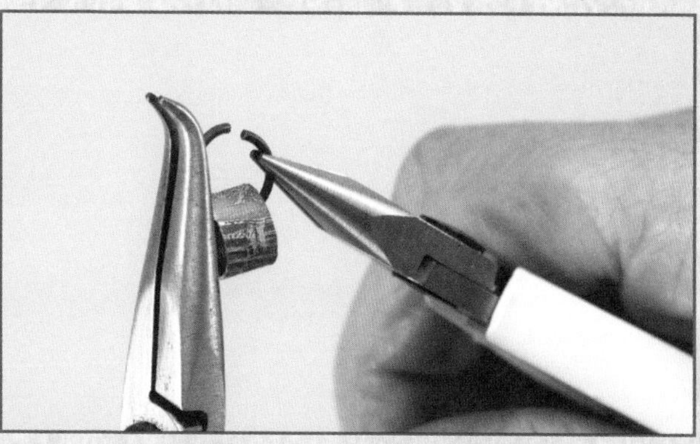

3 Create First Link
Open a jump ring. Add a piece of cut tubing to it. Close the jump ring (see *Opening and Closing Jump Rings*, page 15).

4 Create Chain

Add the tube link from step 4, along with a second piece of tubing, to another jump ring. Close the jump ring. Continue building the chain in this manner—one jump ring—one tube until all eleven tube links have been used. There should be five jump rings remaining. Join them together and then attach them to the eleventh tube link (see the main project photo for clarification).

5 Create Bead Dangles

Place one bead cap and one gold bead onto each of six brass headpins. Place one bead cap and one gray pearl onto each of six headpins.

Create a loop at the top of each gold and each gray bead using round-nose pliers. Place the dangles aside.

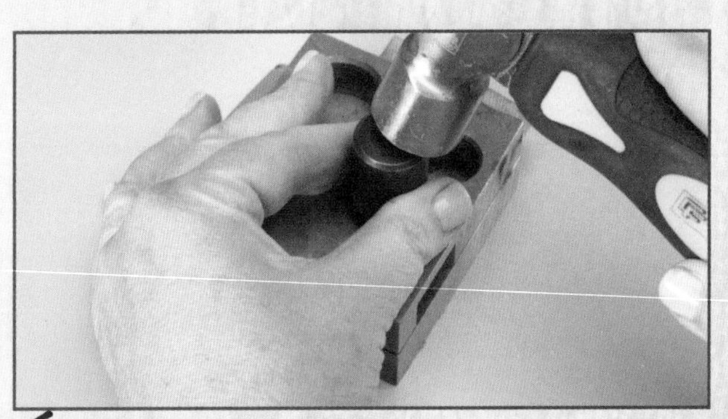

6 Create Circle Charms

Using a circle cutter and a hammer, create two ⅞" (22mm) circles and one ¾" (19mm) circle from the etched brass. (*See Using a Circle Cutter*, page 18.) In the same manner, cut three ½" circles from the etched copper (we had pretty etched hearts in the copper we used and we made a point to capture the hearts inside our ½" (13mm) circles. Repeat this process with the nickel silver, cutting three ⅜" (9mm) circles.

7 Dome Nickel Silver Circles

Place one nickel silver circle into the doming block and shape the circle using a dapper. (See *Using a Dapping Block/Doming a Circle*, page 18.) Remove the circle, place it in a smaller round, and continue dapping to increase the doming on the circle. Repeat this process for the remaining nickel silver circles.

8 Drill Circles

At the top center of each of the circles (including the domed circles), drill a small hole using a drill and $\frac{1}{16}$" drill bit.

9 Create Domed Dangles

Onto each of the remaining three brass headpins place one bead cap followed by one 2mm pearl. Place the wire of the headpin through the drilled hole in the domed nickel silver charm, threading it through the front of the charm. Begin bending the wire into a loop shape.

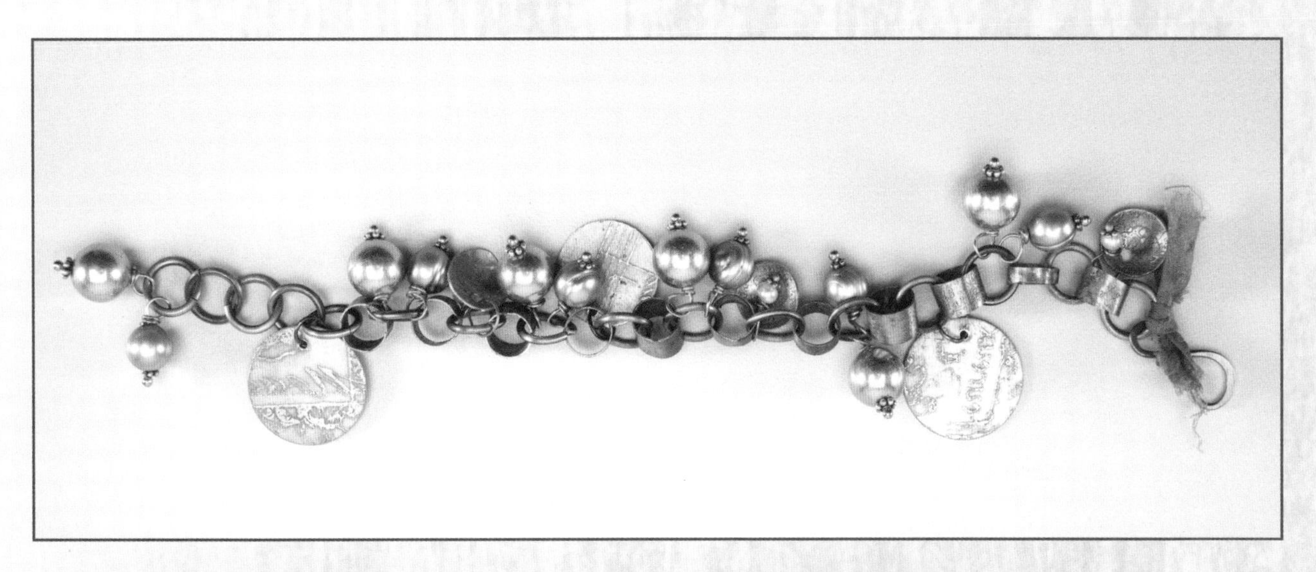

10 Add Bead Dangles to Chain

Arrange the chain so that the end with the five joined jump rings is on your left.

Place the loop of one gold bead dangle onto the last jump ring. Wrap the wire to close the loop. Repeat with one gray pearl dangle.

11 Attach Bead Dangles

Working from right to left, attach one gold bead dangle and one gray bead dangle to the third jump ring. Then attach one gold bead dangle and one gray bead dangle to every other jump ring.

12 Attach Circle Charms to Chain

Continue to work from right to left: open one 5mm jump ring, add one ⅞" (22mm) brass circle charm and one copper charm. Repeat with the remaining 5mm jump rings and charms. Add one charm jump ring to the fourth jump ring in the chain. Add the next charm jump ring to the eighth jump ring in the chain. Add the final charm jump ring to the twelfth jump ring in the chain. Close all three charm jump rings.

13 Attach Domed Circles

Continue to work from right to left: attach one of the domed dangles to the sixth jump ring. Wrap the headpin wire around the base of the loop and trim any excess wire. Repeat this process with the remaining domed circle, attaching it to the tenth jump ring in the chain.

14 Create and Attach Clasp

Create a hook (see *Make a Hook/Clasp*, page 17). Open the jump ring on the right end of the bracelet, add the hook and then close the jump ring.

15 Add Ribbon

Tie a small piece of gray silk ribbon onto the jump ring that holds the hook.

BELOVED NECKLACE

Inspired by the beauty of a beloved evening sunset, this piece pays homage to the amazing process of the sun gracefully cascading away from the day. Cold joining is the key to the layers of this dimensional piece, composed of an array of metals and custom links.

WHAT YOU'LL NEED

METAL, ETCHED AND RESHAPED:
annealed steel wire, 18-gauge

brass jump rings, 18-gauge, 5mm, 18

copper, 22-gauge, 3" × 1" (8cm × 25mm)

nickel silver, 24-gauge 4" × 4" (10cm × 10cm)

steel jump ring, 18-gauge, 8mm, 1

JEWELRY TOOLKIT:
ball-peen hammer

bench block

brass screws, 2 and nuts, 2

center punch tool

circle cutter

flat-nose pliers

forming pliers

SAWING TOOLKIT:
drill and 1⁄16" bit

tin snips

SHAPING & FILING TOOLKIT:
jeweler's file

sandpaper

OTHER:
wood block

1 Create Round Links and Rectangular Chain Links
With a ¼" (6mm) circle punch, create ten copper discs. File edges as needed (see *Using a Circle Cutter*, page 18). From the etched nickel silver cut eight ½" × 1" (13mm × 25mm) long links.

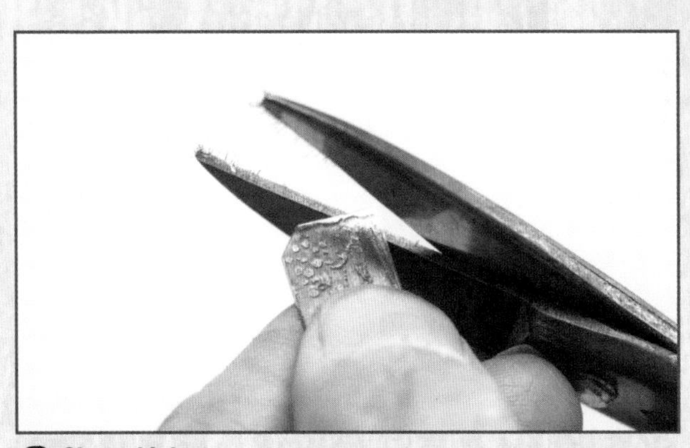

2 Shape Links
With tin snips, round the four corners of each link. If needed, file any rough edges. With sandpaper, smooth the edges of each link.

3 Mark and Drill Holes
Near the top and bottom of each link (the rectangular links and the discs), use a center punch tool to create a guide for the drill. With a drill fitted with a 1⁄16" drill bit, drill one hole into the top and bottom of each link.

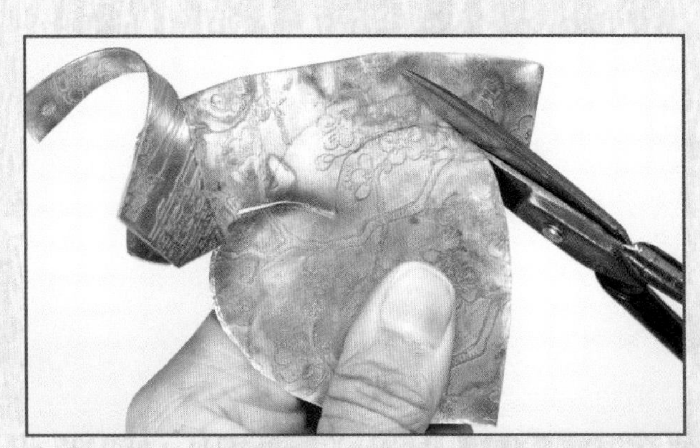

4 Cut Out the Heart
Using tin snips, cut out a basic heart shape from etched nickel silver.

5 Form Heart

Lay the heart onto a wood block and shape the metal with the ball end of a ball-peen hammer. The goal is to form a gentle curve.

6 Cut Copper Banner

As in step 4, cut out a banner shape from the etched copper. Be sure the length of the banner spans the width of the heart. File any rough edges.

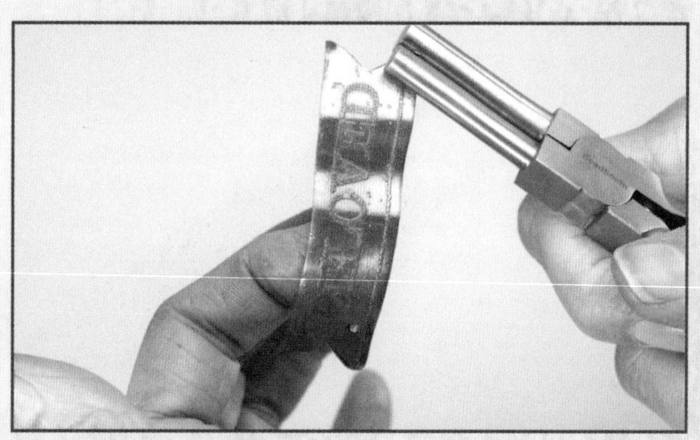

7 Form Banner

Using forming pliers, create ripples along the length of the banner.

8 Prepare and Drill Holes in Heart and Banner

Using a Sharpie, create guides for attaching the banner to the heart.

Using a drill fitted with a 1/16" drill bit create guide holes—going through both the banner and the heart.

Drill holes for the chain on each side of the top of the heart.

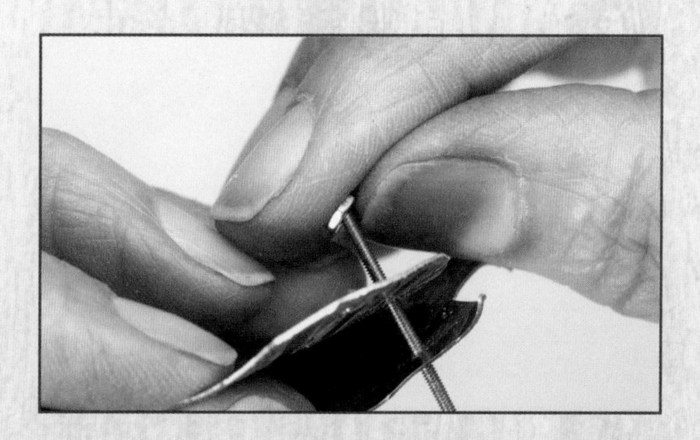

9 Insert Screw Through Heart and Banner

Working from the front of the banner, insert the screw through the banner and then through the front of the corresponding side of the heart. Place a nut onto the back of the screw and tighten the nut using flat-nose pliers. Repeat on the other side of the banner.

10 Trim Screws

Using wire cutters or metal shears, trim the screws so they extend about ⅛" (3mm) beyond the nuts.

11 Dap Screws

With a ball-peen hammer, dap screws until they are flat.

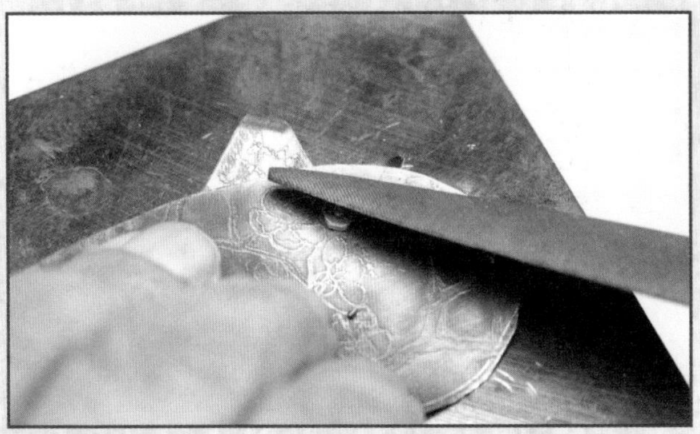

12 File Screws

File the screws to remove any sharp edges.

13 Creating Clasp

Cut a 4½ " (11cm) piece of 18-gauge annealed steel wire. Sand the wire with 200-grit sandpaper to remove any finish. Hammer one end of the wire with the flat end of a ball-peen hammer until it resembles a flat paddle.

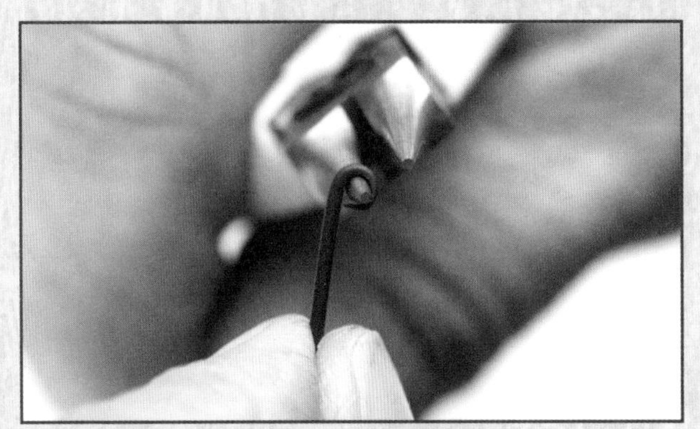

14 Create a Loop in Paddle End of Wire

Cut a loop at one end of the wire using round-nose pliers. Bend the paddle end over needle-nose pliers to create a tiny oval loop.

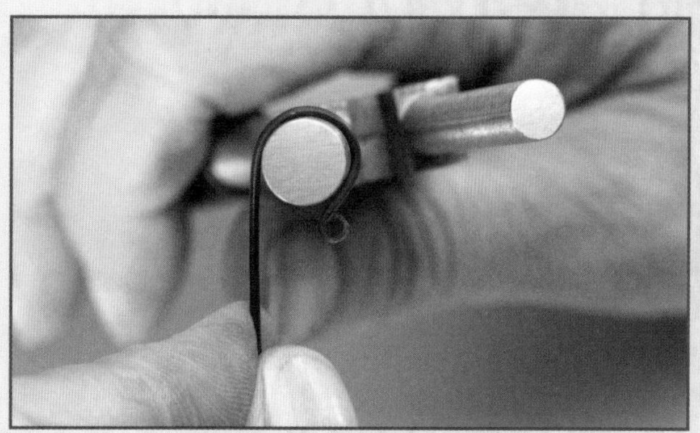

15 Create Larger Loop Behind the First Loop

Using forming pliers, create an 8mm loop directly beneath the tiny loop.

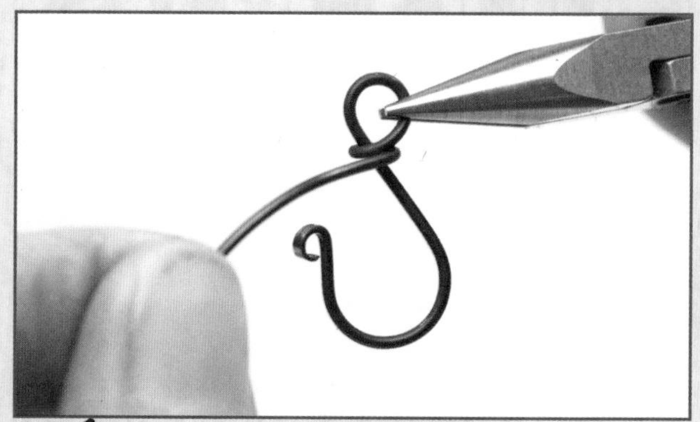

16 Create Second Loop and Wrap Wire

Create a second loop at the base of the large loop. Wrap the wire tail around this loop to close it, then trim any excess wire.

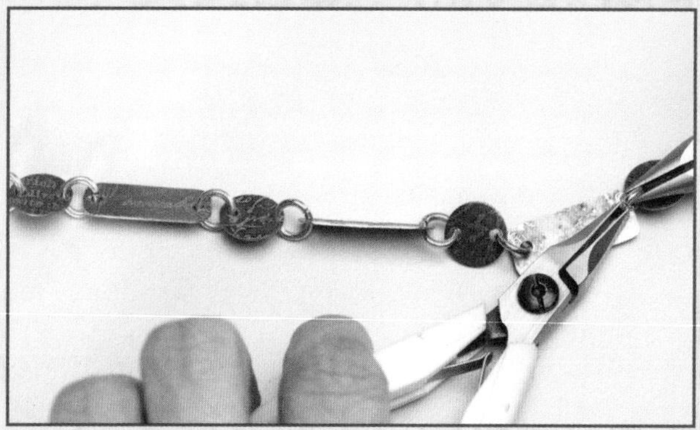

17 Build Chain

Attach one disc to each of the jump rings. Add a rectangular link to the same jump ring and then close the ring (see *Opening and Closing Jump Rings*, page 15). Continue building the chain by attaching a second jump ring followed by one rectangular link to the other hole in the disc. Continue in this manner until you have a piece of chain consisting of five discs, four rectangular links and eight jump rings. Make another piece of chain exactly like this one.

18 Create Holes for Chain and Attach Chain

Place one jump ring through one of the holes created at the top of the heart. To this jump ring, attach one side of the chain and close it. Repeat this process on the other side of the heart.

19 Attach Clasp to Chain

Open the brass jump ring at the end of one of the pieces of chain and slide on the clasp. Close the jump ring. To the jump ring on the other end piece of chain, attach the steel jump ring and close it.

TIPS

DARKENING AND ADDING PATINAS

Darkening solution will bring out the layers of etching and add depth to your piece. See *Darkening and Adding Patinas*, pages 20–21, for more information on how to do this.

BEHOLDING THE PAST PHOTO WRAP BRACELET

One thing that remains a constant throughout our designs is the nod to the history that has created who we are today. Carrying our past with us is not only of great importance but it also insures our stories and our heritage will be passed down for generations to come. I love that with this bracelet we are able to create a piece that incorporates a bit of family history.

WHAT YOU'LL NEED

METAL, ETCHED AND RESHAPED:
brass, 22-gauge

nickel silver, scrap

OTHER METAL:
brass, unetched

brass jump rings, 5mm, 2

steel jump rings, 10mm, 2

JEWELRY TOOL KIT:
ball-peen hammer

bench block

doming block and dappers

SHAPING & FILING TOOLKIT:
jeweler's file

rawhide mallet

SAWING KIT:
circle cutter

drill and 1⁄16" bit

jeweler's saw and #2 blade

wood block or bench pin

BEADS & FINDINGS STASH:
opaque crystals, 2mm, 4

pink potato pearls, 7mm, 14

purchased clasp

pyrite beads, 7mm, 2

pyrite beads, 15mm, 4

topaz briolettes, 8mm, 3

FABRIC & SEWING STASH:
blue satin ribbon, 5" × ½" (13cm × 13mm)

brown silk shantung, 16" × ½" (41cm × 13mm)

cream embroidery floss

taupe thread

taupe velvet ribbon, 16" × ¼" (41cm × 6mm)

OTHER:
brass headpin

bronze wire, 18 gauge

darkening solution

desaturated alcohol

embroidery needle

griddle

iron

paper towels

photo

round-nose pliers

sewing machine

toner transparency

tweezers

To Make the Photo Charm

1 Make Photo Test Print

Print a high-quality, high-contrast photo onto regular paper. Testing on regular paper will give you an idea of what kind of contrast you can expect. You can continue to test print until you achieve the desired contrast level. Lighten or darken the image, reprint and evaluate until you are satisfied.

TIPS: PRINTING

- If you are using a color photo, convert the photo to black and white with black at the highest value (contrast) possible.
- Start with images no larger than 3" × 3" (8cm × 8cm) in size.

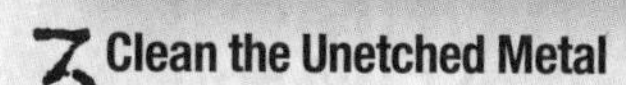

2 Print Final Image Onto Transparency

The photo must be printed onto a photocopy transparency. Be sure to use a toner printer, not an ink-jet printer. Only the ink from a toner printer will work for this technique.

3 Clean the Unetched Metal

See *Preparing the Metal for Etching*, page 10.

4 Prepping the Image

Heat the iron to the highest setting possible and heat the griddle to 400°F (200°C). Place a paper towel on the griddle.

Place a drop of desaturated alcohol on both the unetched metal and the transparency. Press the image onto the metal while both are still wet. Make sure the printed side of the transparency is against the metal.

5 Heating Metal

Place the metal image side up on the paper towel. Cover the metal with a second paper towel. Place the iron on top of the paper towel for two minutes.

Remove the iron and top layer of paper towel. With a pair of tweezers, lift the metal and allow it to cool for one minute.

TIPS

SUCCESSFUL HEAT TRANSFER TIPS

If the metal gets too hot, the image will smear. If the iron is too cool, the image will not transfer at all. Always ensure the iron has heated for at least ten minutes or until the preheat light is off. The same holds true for the griddle. If you are using an iron with an automatic shutoff, watch closely and reheat completely if necessary.

6 Removing Transparency
Lift the edge of the transparency and with tweezers pull it slowly away from the metal. Then etch the metal as per usual instructions (see *How to Etch Metal*, pages 8–13).

7 Cut Out the Photo
Using a jeweler's saw and a #2 saw blade, cut around the perimeter of the photo (in this case, we cut the metal to a size of ¾" × 1" [19mm × 25mm]). (See *Using a Jeweler's Saw*, page 19.)

8 Saw Metal Tabs
Using a jeweler's saw and #2 blade, cut two tabs from the etched brass. Cut one to measure 1" × ½" (25mm × 13mm) and the other ½" × ¼" (13mm × 6mm).

9 Create Discs
With a circle cutter, punch discs from the remaining etched copper: three ½" (13mm) discs and one ⅜" (9mm) disc. Punch one ½" (13mm) disc from the nickel silver scrap. (See *Using a Circle Cutter*, page 18.)

10 File Edges
With a jeweler's file, file the edges of all the metal pieces and round the corners of the photo charm.

11 Drill Holes
With a drill fitted with a 1⁄16" drill bit, drill one hole in the photo charm near the center of the top edge. Drill one hole in each of the discs, again, near an edge.

12 Dome Silver Nickel Disc
Place the nickel silver disc into the 1" (25mm) round of a dapping block. Using a dapper and hammer, hammer the disc until it begins to form a cup, moving the dapper in a circular motion as you work. Once the disc begins to dome, switch to a smaller dapper and keep the disc in the same large round. Once the sides begin to cup toward the top of the round, move the disc into a smaller round and repeat the process until the desired shape is achieved. (See *Using a Dapping Block/Doming a Circle,* page 18.)

To Make the Fabric Band

13 Begin Sewing Wrap
Place an 18" (46cm) piece of velvet ribbon on top of an 8" (20cm) piece of fabric in a contrasting color. Line up the ends of the two, and sew them together with a running stitch to make a strap. Since the ribbon is longer than the fabric, there will be an extra 10" (25cm) of ribbon hanging from the fabric after they've been stitched together.

14 Add Jump Rings to Strap
Draw two 10mm jump rings onto velvet portion of strap. Lay the velvet flat on top of the fabric strap and fold the two pieces in half. Pull one jump ring into the new fold on the adjacent side. Fold entire strap in half.

15 Sew Ribbon Band
Place the now folded ribbon and fabric strap into the sewing machine and stitch the layers together.

16 Hide Ribbon Band Stitching
Fold the excess velvet ribbon over the fabric strap. Place the remaining velvet ribbon over the folded piece and stitch closed. Continue stitching through all layers.

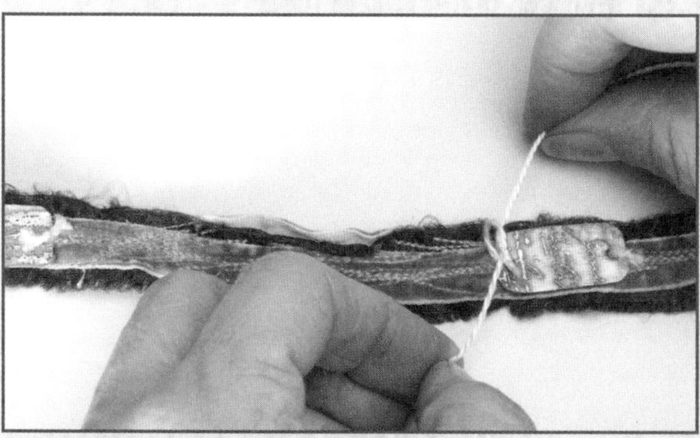

17 Attach Etched Tabs
Using embroidery floss and a needle, sew each of the tabs to the front of the ribbon band, taking care to space them evenly.

18 Make Dangles and Attach to Band
Place one 7mm pearl onto a brass headpin. Create a loop and wrap to close. Place one 7mm pyrite bead onto a headpin. Create a loop and wrap to close. Position a 1½" (4cm) piece of blue ribbon under the ribbon band. Thread the two bead dangles onto the ribbon.

To Make the Chain

19 Attach Photo Charm to Band

Slide a 5mm brass jump ring through the hole drilled at the top of the photo charm and close the ring (see *Opening and Closing Jump Rings*, page 15). Slide the jump ring onto the ribbon band and double knot the ribbon to secure.

20 Begin Chain

Cut one 4" (10cm) piece of 24-gauge bronze wire and create a loop using round-nose pliers. Place the loop through the jump ring at the end of the ribbon band and wrap the loop to close. Place one 7mm pink pearl onto the open end of the wire. Create a new loop and close. Continue in this manner until you have a chain consisting of two pearls, one pyrite bead, three more pearls and one closed brass jump ring.

21 Create Adjacent Chain

As you did in step 20, and starting from the jump ring on the opposite end of the band, create a chain consisting of six 7mm pink pearls, followed by two15mm pyrite beads, one 7mm pearl, one 15mm pyrite bead and one 7mm pearl.

22 Create Clasp

Cut a 1" (25mm) piece of 18-gauge bronze wire. At one end of the wire, use round-nose pliers to turn a loop. Wrap the wire tail around a ½" (13mm) dowel. (See *Making a Hook/Clasp*, page 17, for a full step-by-step demonstration.) Place the open loop through the ending link of the chain and wrap the remaining wire to close it. Insert the hook into the brass jump ring on the other piece of chain to close and secure the bracelet.

23 Add Ribbon to Jump Rings

Tie a 1½" (4cm) piece of blue ribbon through the jump ring at each end of the ribbon band.

24 Attach Disc

Open one 5mm brass jump ring and slide it through the drilled hole on one of the ½" (13mm) discs. Place this jump ring through the jump ring on one end of the ribbon band and close it. Repeat this process on the other end of the ribbon band.

25 Create Topaz Dangle

Place one topaz briolette onto a brass headpin. Using round-nose pliers, create a loop and slide the loop onto the first jump ring from step 24. Close the jump ring.

26 Attach Bead Dangles on Opposite End of Band

To the opposite end of the ribbon band, attach two bead dangles: one with a pyrite bead and the other with a topaz briolette.

27 Create Dangles With Beads and Discs

Place one 2mm crystal bead onto each of three headpins. Create a loop in each using round-nose pliers, and place one disc onto each loop.

28 Add Dangles to Bracelet

Attach one bead dangle through the loop of the pyrite link on the left side, and wrap the wire to close the loop. On the opposite side of the bracelet, slide one bead dangle through the loop of the third pearl and close the loop. The remaining dangle should be added to the bracelet between the fifth and sixth pearls.

29 Create and Add Domed Dangle

Place one crystal bead onto the remaining headpin. With round-nose pliers, create a loop. Place the domed disc onto the headpin. Place the loop through the closed jump ring at the end of the chain and wrap the loop closed.

MAIDEN BY THE SEA EARRINGS

The delicate yet assertive nature of these earrings was inspired by a fair maiden living within the walls of a fortress by the sea. With a few new techniques and the addition of brilliant stones, nickel silver becomes something richer. Darkener brings out the purity of the etching while handmade ear wires add an additional skill to your arsenal of techniques.

You will find templates for *Maiden by the Sea* on page 122. You can also print them out directly from the *Making Etched Metal Jewelry* companion page. Visit CreateMixedMedia.com/MEMJ-companion.

WHAT YOU'LL NEED

METAL, ETCHED AND RESHAPED:
nickel silver, 22-gauge

OTHER METAL:
silver wire, 20-gauge

steel jump rings, 3mm, 2

steel wire, 24-gauge

JEWELRY TOOLKIT:
ball-peen hammer

butane torch

chain-nose pliers

chemical brush

doming block and dappers

firing block

flat-nose pliers with protective handles

flux

forming pliers (7mm)

rawhide hammer

round-nose pliers

solder

wire cutters

SAWING KIT:
bench pin

center punch tool

circle cutter

drill and 1/16" bit

jeweler's saw and #2 saw blade

rubber cement

wood block

SHAPING & FILING TOOLKIT:
metal file

BEADS & FINDINGS STASH:
crystal briolettes, 8mm, 4

OTHER:
bowl with cold water

cotton balls

darkening solution

soap and water

steel wool

tweezers

1 Using Flower Template
Trace the template and, using rubber cement, affix it to the nickel silver sheet metal.

2 Sawing Flower
Using a jeweler's saw with a #2 blade and a bench pin, cut the shape from the nickel silver (see *Using a Jeweler's Saw*, page 19). Repeat to cut out a second flower.

3 Removing Template Paper
Remove the paper from the flower shape and gently remove any rubber cement residue.

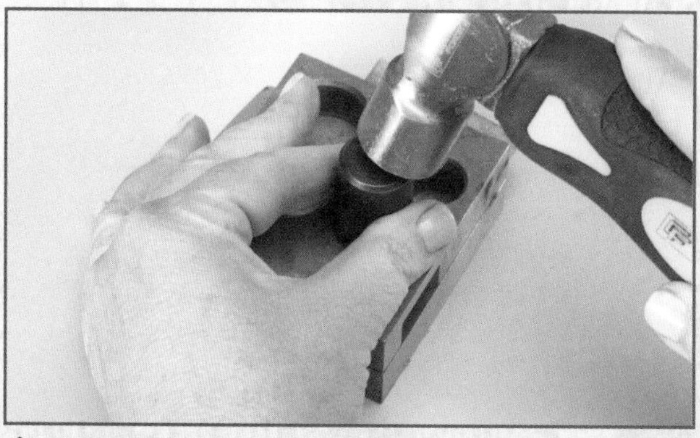

4 Cutting Discs
With the remaining nickel silver, create four discs using a ½" (13mm) circle cutter (see *Using a Circle Cutter*, page 18) and a ball-peen hammer.

5 Drilling Holes
Using a center punch tool, create a dimple to use at the top of the center petal as a drilling guide. Create three dimples at the bottom of the bottom petal. Drill through all guides. Repeat on the second flower. Create guides on the top and bottom of two of the discs and drill.

6 Doming Discs

Place one of the remaining nickel silver discs into a doming block and shape the disc using a dapper and a rawhide hammer, until it is cup-shaped (see *Using a Dapping Block/Doming a Circle*, page 18). Remove the circle and place it in a smaller round to increase the doming. Repeat this process with the remaining disc.

7 Apply Flux

Apply flux to both the center of the flower and the bottom of the domed cup.

8 Solder Cup to Flower

Cut ¼" (6mm) of solder and place it onto the center of the flower. Activate the torch. Hold the cup over the solder until the solder fuses to the domed cup. Repeat steps 7 and 8 for the remaining flower.

9 Cool and Quench

Let the pieces cool for five minutes, then quench them: With tweezers lift the still-hot metal and place it into a bowl of cold water. Then remove the metal from the water and dry it with a soft cloth.

10 Clean Soldered Pieces

Clean off excess flux and heat scale with steel wool. Rinse the pieces with soap and water.

11 Darken Soldered Pieces

Place darkening solution onto a cotton ball and apply it to the metal. Buff the metal with steel wool to create definition.

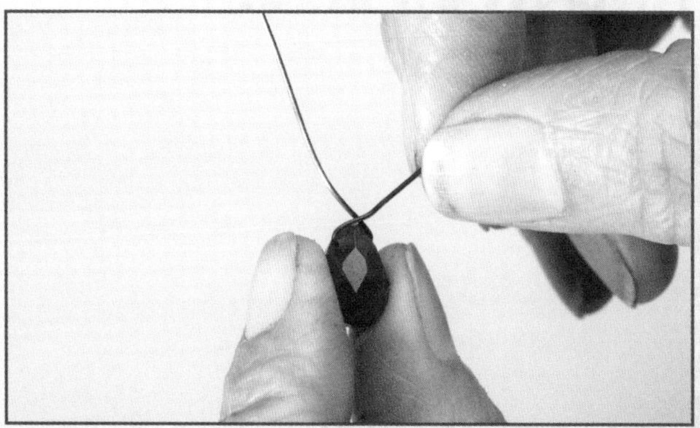

12 Attach Beads

Cut three 4" (10cm) pieces of 24-gauge steel wire. Place one piece of wire through the center of a crystal briolette. Fold the two ends of the wire together until they meet.

13 Secure Bead to Metal Flower

Wrap one end of the tail around the top of the briolette. Create a loop with round-nose pliers and place the loop through the center hole. Wrap the loop closed and trim excess wire. Repeat steps 12–13 with the remaining beads.

14 Attaching Round Disc

Attach one 3mm jump ring to the top drilled hole of the main part of the earring (see *Opening and Closing Jump Rings*, on page 15). Close the jump ring and repeat for the remaining earring.

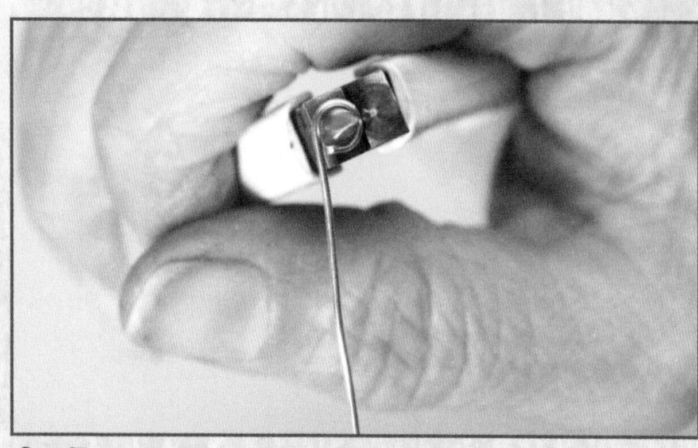

15 Creating Ear Wire

Cut two 1½" (4cm) pieces of 20-gauge silver wire. File the end of the wire to smooth it and remove any burrs. Using round-nose pliers, create a small loop at one end of the wire.

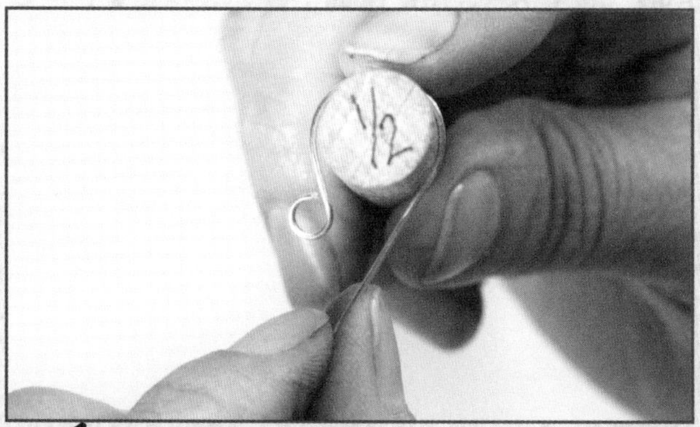

16 Finish Ear Wire

Place the loop end of the wire into 7mm forming pliers or onto a dowel, and wrap the wire. With chain-nose pliers, create a small bend ¼" (6mm) from the end of the wire. File any rough edges on the ends of the wires.

17 Attach Ear Wire

Open the small loop of the ear wire and place it through the top hole of the disc. Close the loop using round-nose pliers. Repeat steps 15–17 for the remaining earring.

OLGA & DOLLIE PICTURE FRAME NECKLACE

Growing up I was blessed to have two great-grandmothers. While Olga was technically a stepmother to my grandmother, through a child's eyes she was a kind person who offered up treats and wonderfully warm knitted slippers and blankets.

My grandmother gifted me with this darling photo of Olga and her sister Dollie many years ago, and it remains a constant in my work today. I adore the two little girls perched on a bench with their hair perfectly coiffed and their pristine white dresses carefully arranged.

A photo such as this is the perfect addition to an etched frame meant to be worn on a hand-crafted chain composed of pyrite and custom links. I can think of no better way to complete the delicate nature of the frame than with a sweet photo. Our hope is you will seek either a current photo or perhaps an heirloom photo to hold close to your heart.

You will find templates for *Olga & Dollie* on page 122. You can also print them out directly from the *Making Etched Metal Jewelry* companion page. Visit CreateMixedMedia.com/MEMJ-companion.

WHAT YOU'LL NEED

METAL, ETCHED AND RESHAPED:
brass, 22-gauge

nickel silver, 22-gauge

OTHER METAL:
brass jump rings, 5mm, 2

brass screws, ½" (13mm), with nuts, 5

brass wire, 18-gauge

JEWELRY TOOLKIT:
ball-peen hammer

bench block

flat-nose pliers

forming pliers

SHAPING & FILING TOOLKIT:
jeweler's file

SAWING KIT:
drill and 1⁄16" bit

jeweler's saw and #2 blade

wood block or bench pin

BEADS & FINDINGS STASH:
pyrite beads, 5mm, round, 2

pyrite beads, 10mm, 6

OTHER:
packing tape

resin kit

vintage photo

1 Cut Out Template Pieces
Adhere the three template pieces to the etched brass and silver, as indicated in the main photo. Using a jeweler's saw fitted with #2 blade, cut out all three pieces and a strip of brass, ½" × 1" (13mm × 25mm). (See *Using a Jeweler's Saw*, page 19.)

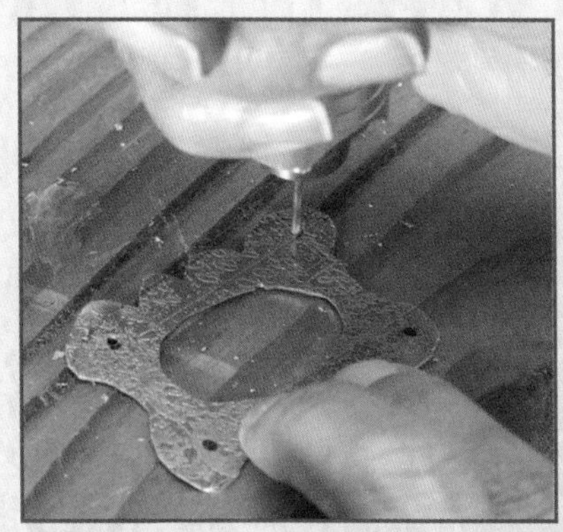

2 Drill Holes
Using a drill fitted with a 1⁄16" bit, drill four holes in the frame front, one in each corner.

3 File Rough Metal Edges
Using a jeweler's file, file the edges of all cut metal pieces until there are no rough or sharp parts.

4 Back Frame Front With Tape
Place a strip of packing tape onto the back of the frame front. Burnish the tape to the metal to ensure a good seal.

5 Pour Resin
Mix resin according to manufacturer's directions. Pour a thin layer of resin into the opening of the frame front. Allow this resin to dry for four hours.

Mix another batch of resin and pour a second layer onto the first. Allow the resin to dry for a full twenty-four hours.

6 Drill Additional Holes

Sandwich the frame and backing together with a binder clip. Using the holes you drilled in step 2 as a guide, drill four holes in the nickel silver frame back.

Drill three more holes in the brass: two near but offset from the two holes at the top and one in the center bottom. Use these three new holes as a guide to drilling similarly placed holes in the nickel silver. There should be seven holes in each piece of metal, and the holes should all line up when the pieces are stacked.

Drill two last holes in the nickel silver frame back near the bottom edge where the nickel silver will peek out from the brass frame front.

Finally, drill two holes in the smaller brass bar—these should line up with the last two you drilled in the nickel silver.

Insert screws in four of the holes as shown. Secure with nuts on the back of the frame.

7 Insert Photo Into Frame

Slide the photo into the frame. Insert and secure the final screw.

8 Dap and Secure Nuts

Trim screw backs, if necessary, and dap screw backs and nuts with the round end of a ball-peen hammer. Add a drop of resin to each to secure permanently and allow the resin to dry completely.

9 Attach Brass Bar

Place one 5mm jump ring through each of the holes in the brass bar. Slide these jump rings through the drilled holes in the frame back. Close the jump rings.

10 Form Links

Cut 10" (25cm) of bronze wire. With a hammer and a bench block, hammer the wire in a random fashion and flatten the ends. Repeat this process eleven times, for a total of twelve pieces of wire.

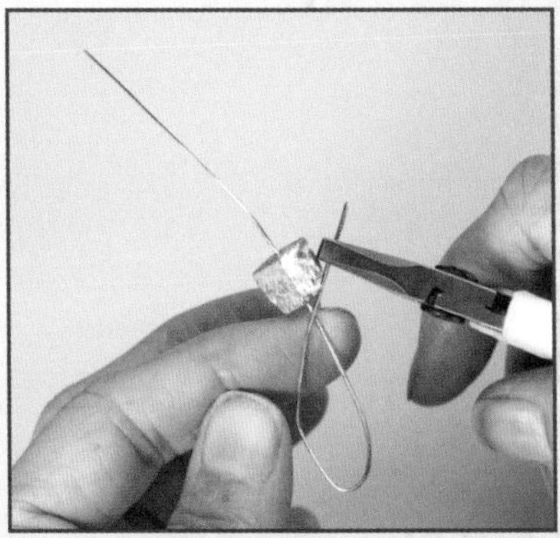

11 Forming Links
Use forming pliers to loosely bend wire 2" (5cm) from the end. Wrap the short tail of the wire around the center of the wire. Add a pyrite bead to the wire.

12 Finish Link
Loosely bend the wire 2" (5cm) from the other end of the wire and wrap.

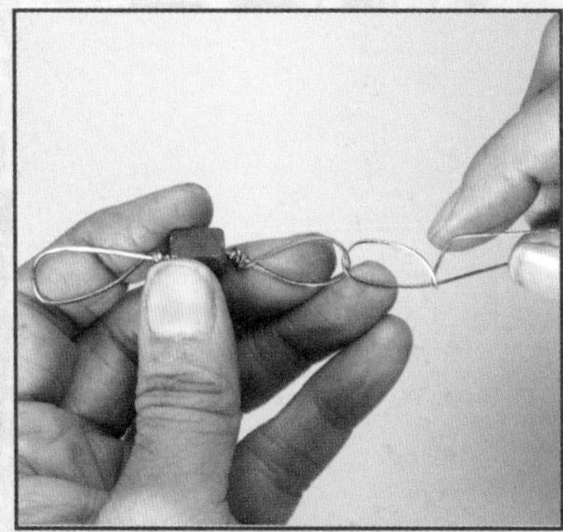

13 Create Chain
Create and add links in the following order: one brass pyrite link, two pyrite links, one brass pyrite link, one pyrite link, three brass links and two pyrite links.

14 Attach Chain to Frame
Double up the chain (fold it in half). Slide the two ending links onto a 10mm jump ring and slide the jump rings though one of the holes at the top of the frame. Close the jump ring.

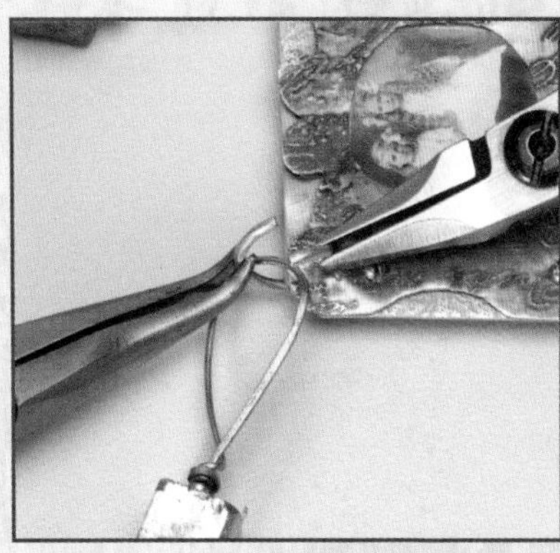

15 Create Final Link and Attach
Make one more pyrite link, as done in steps 11 and 12, then attach it to the frame as in step 14.

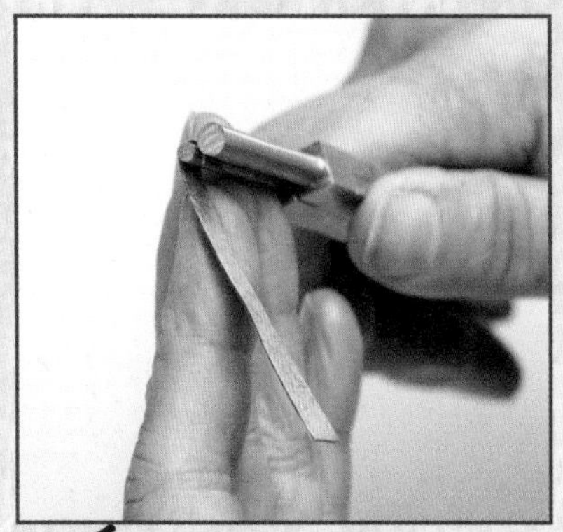

16 Begin Forming Clasp
Bend one end of the ¼" × 1" (6mm × 25mm) brass strip around the smaller barrel of the forming pliers until a closed curl forms.

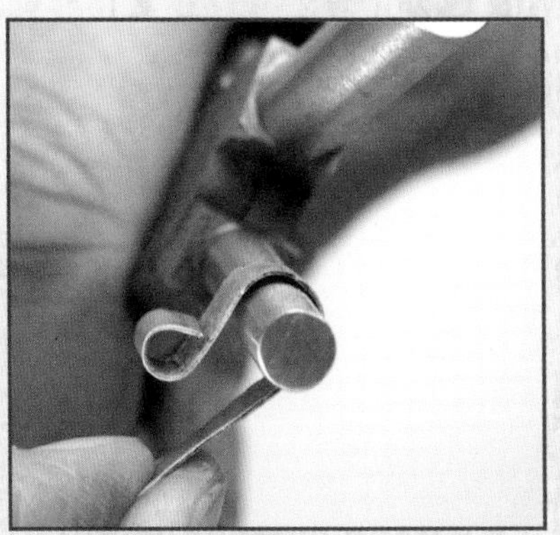

17 Continue Clasp
Make another, larger curl directly behind the first, bending the brass in the opposite direction.

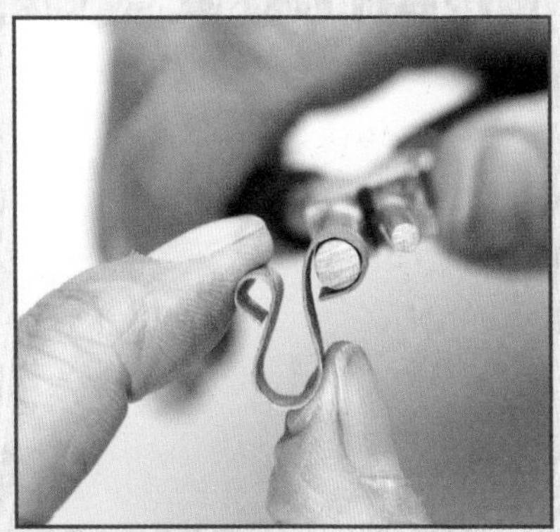

18 Finish Clasp
On the other end of the strip, make another closed curl.

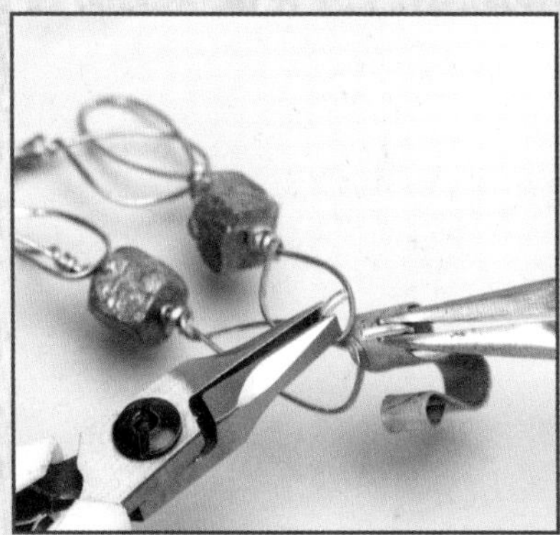

19 Attach Chain to Clasp
Slide the open loops of the chain through a jump ring, then slide the jump ring through the larger link of the finished clasp. Close the jump ring.

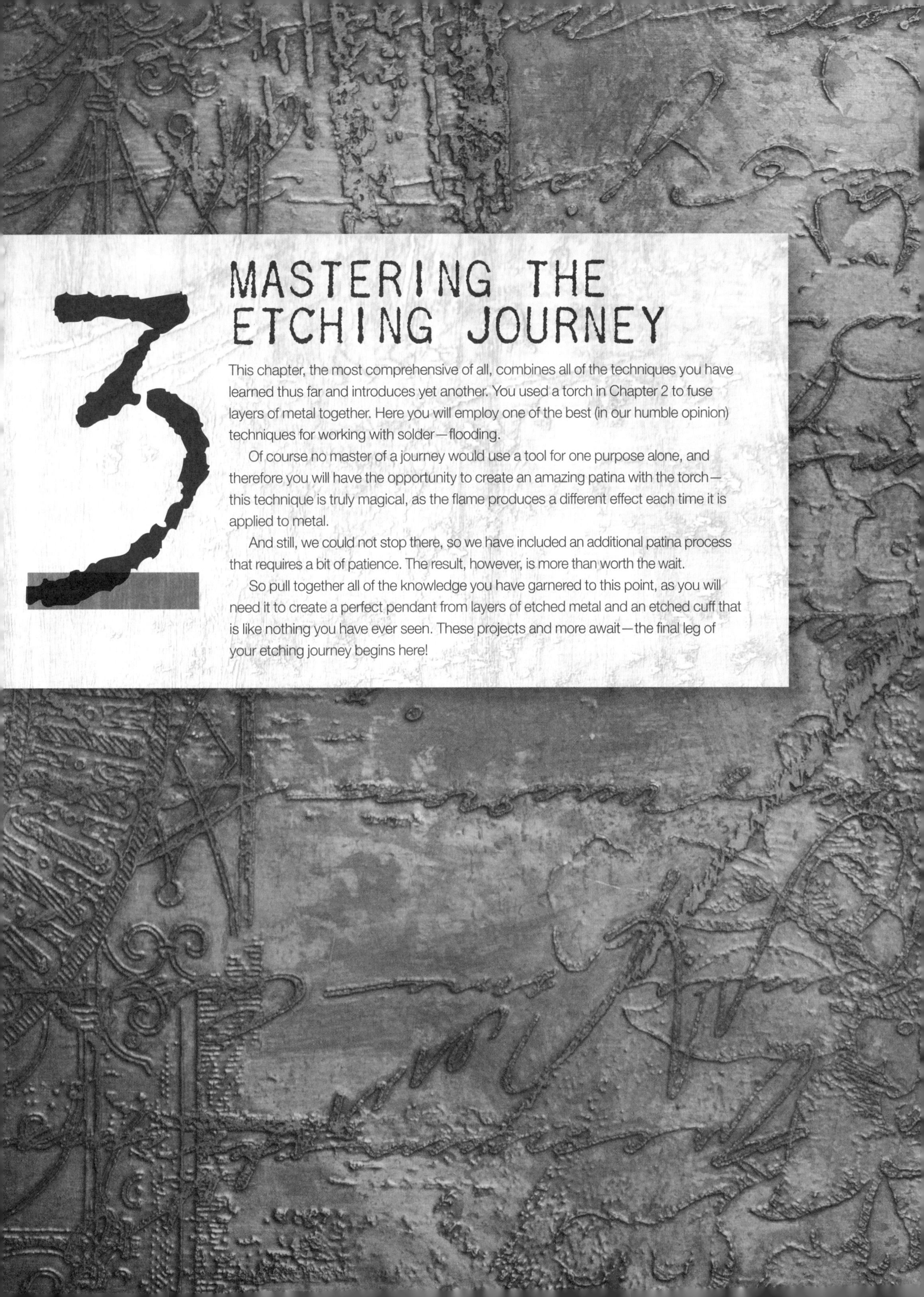

3 MASTERING THE ETCHING JOURNEY

This chapter, the most comprehensive of all, combines all of the techniques you have learned thus far and introduces yet another. You used a torch in Chapter 2 to fuse layers of metal together. Here you will employ one of the best (in our humble opinion) techniques for working with solder—flooding.

Of course no master of a journey would use a tool for one purpose alone, and therefore you will have the opportunity to create an amazing patina with the torch—this technique is truly magical, as the flame produces a different effect each time it is applied to metal.

And still, we could not stop there, so we have included an additional patina process that requires a bit of patience. The result, however, is more than worth the wait.

So pull together all of the knowledge you have garnered to this point, as you will need it to create a perfect pendant from layers of etched metal and an etched cuff that is like nothing you have ever seen. These projects and more await—the final leg of your etching journey begins here!

WRAPPED TREASURES FABRIC TOOL WRAP

Tools are so very important to creating. That's why it's essential to keep our tools, much like treasure, in a safe place. While a standard toolbox or tool wrap is all well and good, a custom tool wrap adorned with an etched and patinated buckle is exciting.

Ruth and I are both of the mindset that it is very important for our tools to work in more than one manner, if at all possible. Thus, while we employ our torches for soldering and the like, we also enjoy the process of creating a heat patina, which produces a magical finish. With Ruth's love of sewing and my love of fabric, we knew this was a perfect marriage of materials. Hence the tool wrap was born.

You will find templates for *Wrapped Treasures* on page 123. You can also print them out directly from the *Making Etched Metal Jewelry* companion page. Visit CreateMixedMedia.com/MEMJ-companion.

WHAT YOU'LL NEED

METAL, ETCHED AND RESHAPED:
copper, 24-gauge, 3" × 3" (8cm × 8cm)

JEWELRY TOOLKIT:
butane torch

firing block

SAWING KIT:
drill and 1⁄16" bit

jeweler's saw and #2 saw blade

metal shears

wood block

SHAPING & FILING TOOLKIT:
jeweler's file

steel wool

FABRIC & SEWING STASH:
cream embroidery floss

embroidery needle

osenberg fabric

red felt

scraps of vintage lace

sewing machine

taupe thread

BEADS & FINDINGS STASH:

mother of pearl buttons, various sizes, 16

OTHER:
microcrystalline wax

rubber cement

soft cloth

1 Prepare Copper for Cutting

Affix the template to the copper with rubber cement.

Drill a hole in the interior of the buckle using a drill fitted with a 1⁄16" drill bit. Make sure the hole you drill is within the area to be cut out.

Open one end of a jeweler's saw, and thread the saw blade through the hole. Lock the blade into the saw frame. (See *Using a Jeweler's Saw*, page 19.)

2 Remove Interior Cutout of Buckle

Carefully saw out the interior of the buckle, following the lines of the template.

Repeat steps 1–2 on the other side of the buckle.

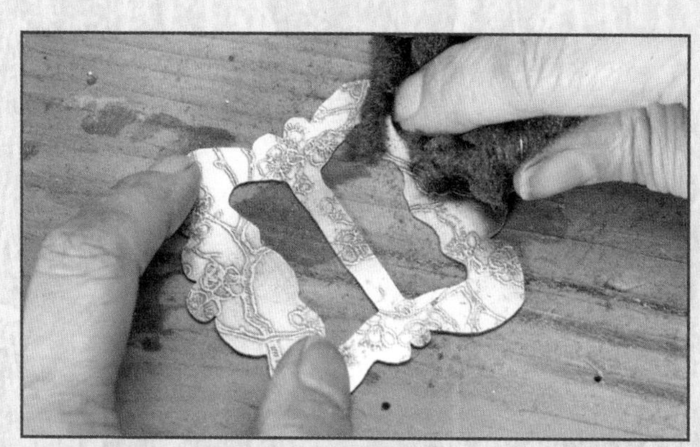

3 File and Smooth Edges

With a jeweler's file, smooth all the edges of the buckle to remove any burrs or sharp edges.

Remove the paper and rubber cement from the buckle. Scrub with steel wool to remove any residue.

4 Drill Holes in Buckle

Using a drill fitted with a 1⁄16" bit, drill holes near the midpoint of the center bar of the buckle.

5 Add Heat Patina

Place the buckle on a firing block. Heat the metal slowly with a butane torch. Stop periodically to check the color of the copper. Moving the torch in slow, steady circles, continue firing until the desired color is achieved. Let the buckle cool for at least ten minutes. Don't rush the cooling step—it's very important.

With a soft cloth, add a layer of microcrystalline wax. Allow the wax to dry completely (another very important step), then add two more layers of wax (see *Darkening and Adding Patinas*, page 20).

TIPS: HEAT PATINA

The heat patina process will typically produce different results each time it is used. The copper will change colors as you heat it, ranging from gold to orange and pink to purple, midnight blue, light blue and then black.

6 Cut Fabric for Exterior of Tool Wrap

Cut a piece of osenberg fabric to measure 17" × 16" (43cm × 41cm).

7 Cut Fabric for Interior of Tool Wrap

Cut a piece of osenberg fabric to measure 11" × 17" (28cm × 43cm). Cut a piece of craft felt to measure 9" × 16" (23cm × 41cm).

8 Cut Pockets

Cut one strip of osenberg fabric to measure 5½" × 16½" (14cm × 42cm) and another strip to 4" × 16½" (10cm × 42cm).

9 Cut Ruffle Strips

Cut three strips of osenberg fabric to measure 2" × 34" (5cm × 86cm).

10 Cut Strap

Cut a strip of osenberg fabric to measure 2½" × 12" (6cm × 13cm). Cut a piece of lace (which will be layered onto the strap fabric) to measure 2" × 5" (5cm × 13cm)

11 Cut Hearts

From a piece of red velvet, cut two hearts, each approximately 1¼" × 1" (3cm × 25mm).

12 Cut Backing for One Heart

From a scrap of lace, cut a heart shape that is approximately 1½" × 1¼" (4cm × 3cm).

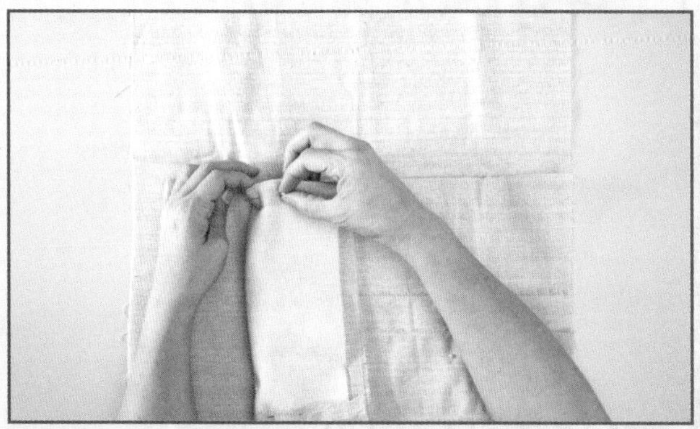

13 Layer Interior Fabric

Lay the piece of felt you cut in step 7 on top of the fabric you cut in step 7. Fold 1" (25mm) of the fabric over the top edge of the felt, and pin it in place. Repeat along the bottom edge of the felt. Lay these pinned pieces together and pin together.

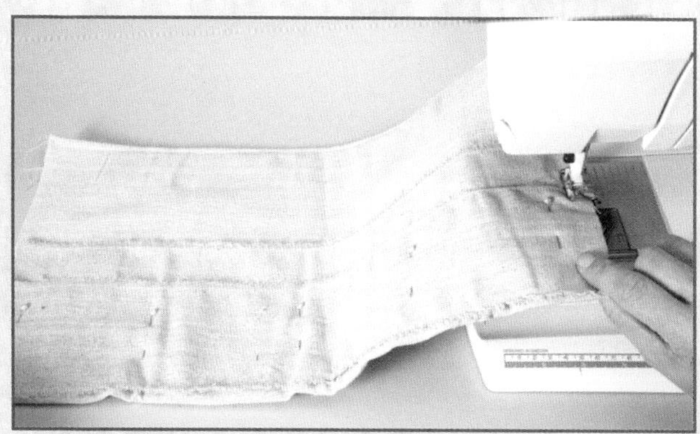

14 Stitch Perimeter of Outer Flap

Place the layered and pinned piece of fabric in your sewing machine, interior side up, and stitch around the entire perimeter.

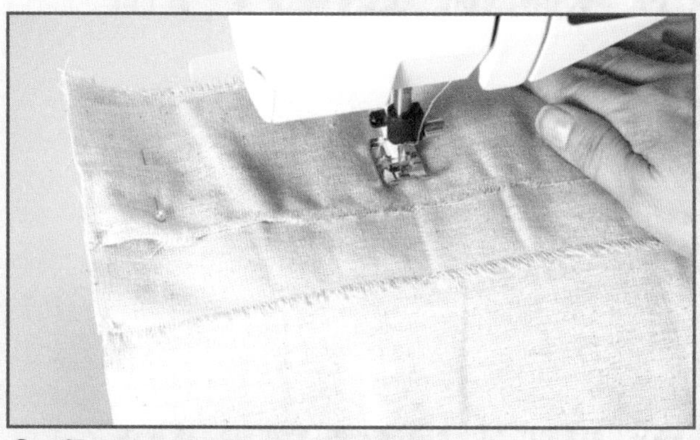

15 Stitch Pockets

Stich in a straight line from the bottom edge to the top of the pocket layer. Do this several times and at various distances to create pockets of varying sizes. Stitch the perimeter of the exterior (¼" [6mm], no fold over—this protects the fabric from fraying beyond the stitch line).

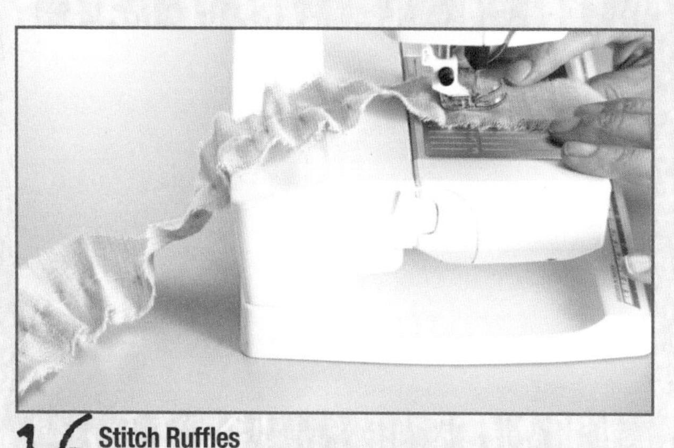

16 Stitch Ruffles

Place a ruffle strip under the presser foot of your sewing machine. Sew with a straight stitch, length set to 5.0, for the entire length of the strip. Leave a tail of 12" (30cm) of thread. Pull one of the threads while pushing the fabric down the other thread to create the ruffle. Repeat with additional strips.

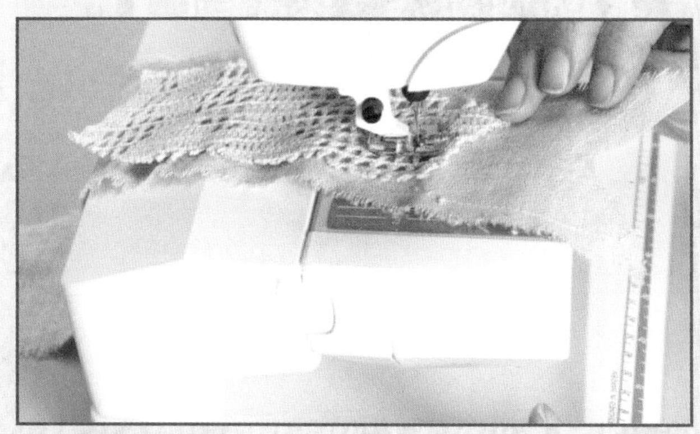

17 Sew Strap

Sew around the perimeter of the strap fabric. Then sew the lace onto the strap, positioning it as shown in the photo.

18 Pin Ruffles and Strap to Exterior

With the exterior of the tool wrap facing up, position the ruffles and the strap and pin them in place.

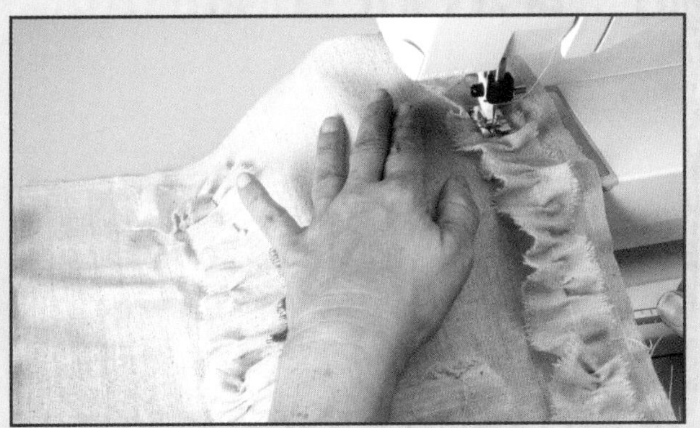

19 Sew Ruffles to Exterior
Using a straight stitch, sew the ruffles onto the fabric.

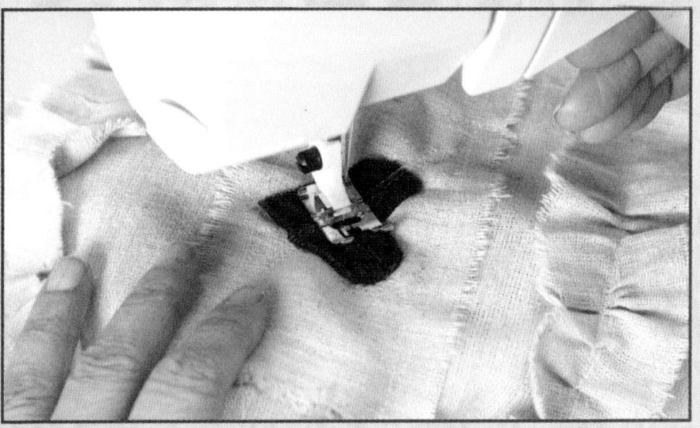

20 Add Heart to Strap
Layer one of the hearts on the strap (pin it in place if necessary). Place the heart under the presser foot and stitch through all layers, stitching around the perimeter of the heart and through the heart if desired.

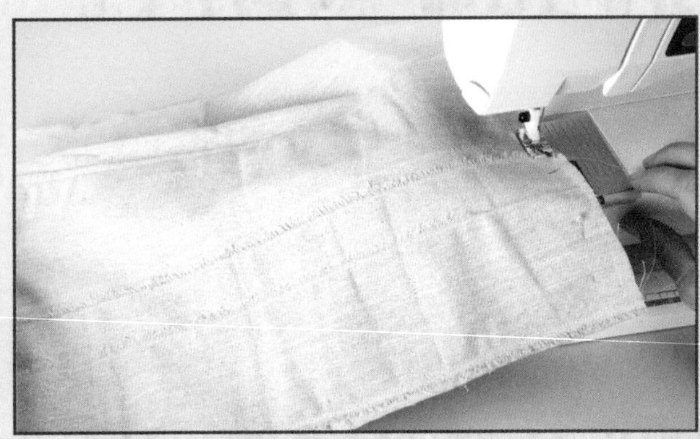

21 Sew Interior and Exterior Together
Place the fabric and felt interior layer on the exterior layer (which should be face down). Sew all four sides of the interior to the exterior, stitching through all layers with taupe thread.

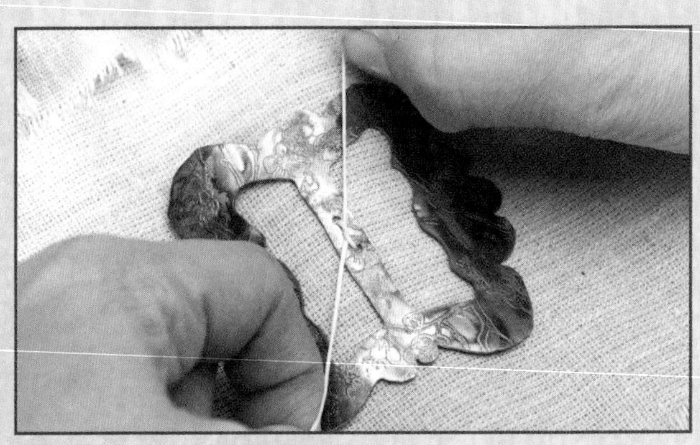

22 Add Buckle to Exterior
With an embroidery needle and floss, sew the buckle to the front of the exterior, about 4½" (11cm) from the right edge of the fabric.

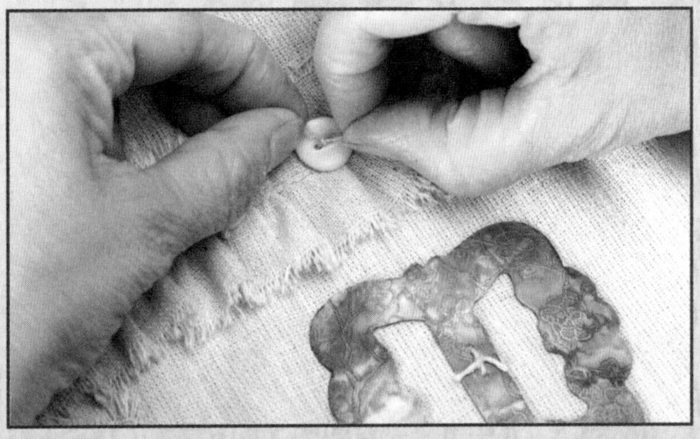

23 Add Buttons
Sew three buttons to the middle ruffle directly above the buckle and three buttons to the bottom ruffle directly below the buckle.

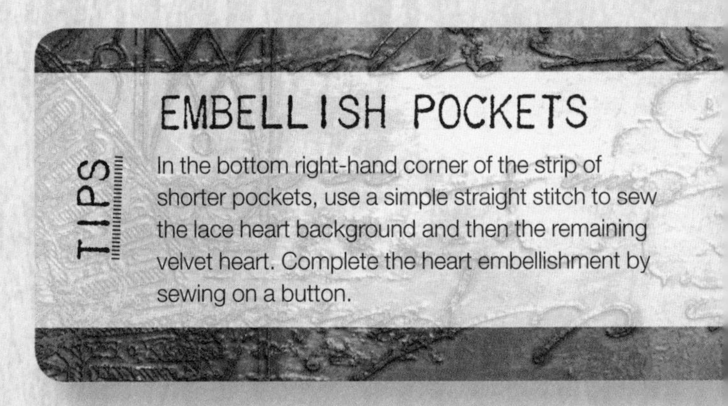

TIPS

EMBELLISH POCKETS

In the bottom right-hand corner of the strip of shorter pockets, use a simple straight stitch to sew the lace heart background and then the remaining velvet heart. Complete the heart embellishment by sewing on a button.

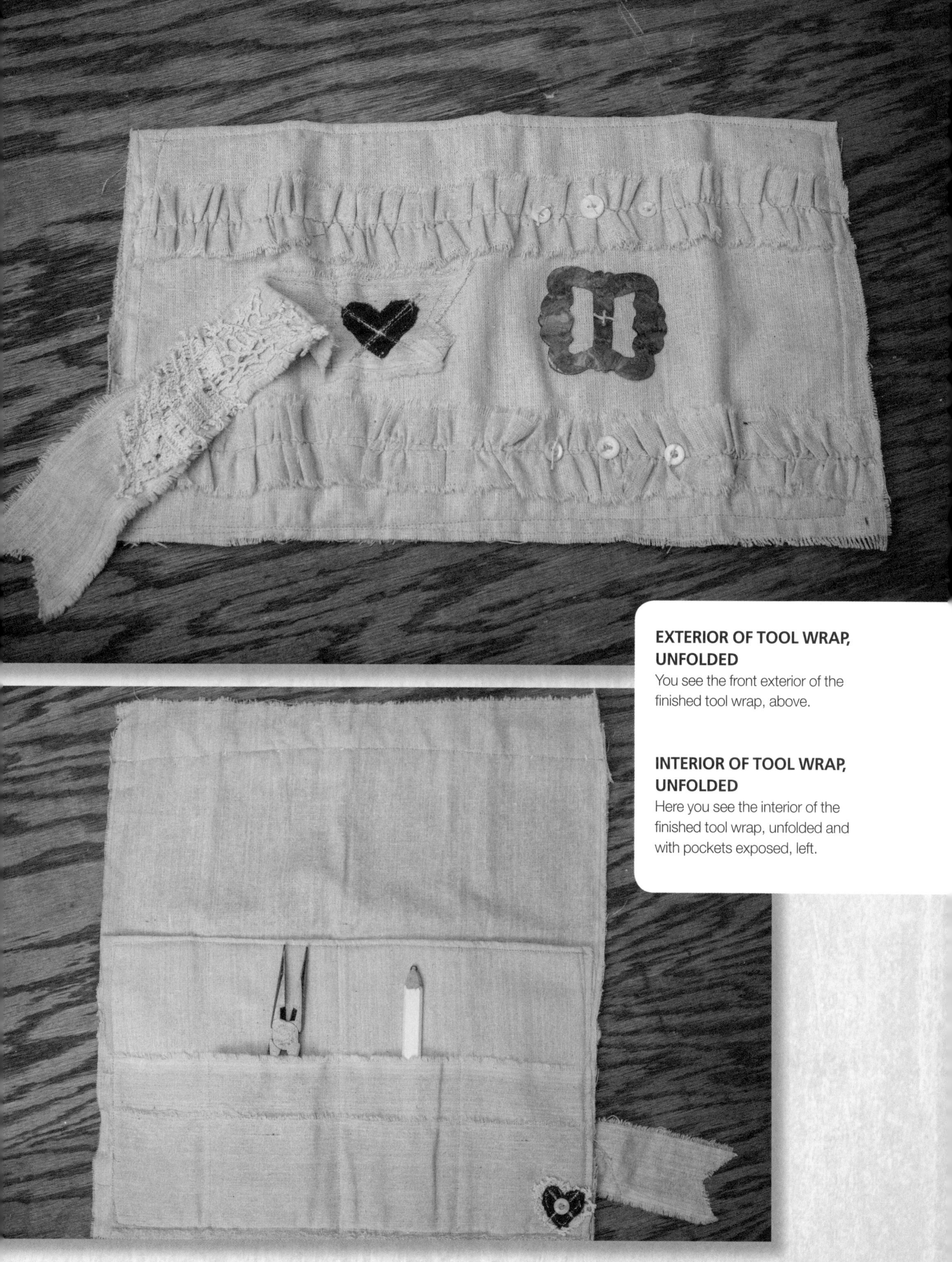

EXTERIOR OF TOOL WRAP, UNFOLDED
You see the front exterior of the finished tool wrap, above.

INTERIOR OF TOOL WRAP, UNFOLDED
Here you see the interior of the finished tool wrap, unfolded and with pockets exposed, left.

HELENA & CONSTANTIUS ETCHED CUFF

According to one tale, the Roman heroine Helena of Constantinople was wearing a bracelet like that of her future husband, Constantius, when they met. Seeing that they donned similar adornments, he declared it was a sign and that they should marry.

Inspired by the Romanesque style that cuffs exude, we sought the perfect Roman heroine to name this project after. It was only after a bit of research that we learned of Helena's story. I can think of no better ode to this tale than a cuff composed of layers of metals, flooded solder and rhinestones.

WHAT YOU'LL NEED

METAL, ETCHED AND RESHAPED:
brass cuff, 1¼" (3cm)
copper, 24-gauge, ¾" × 4¼" (19mm × 11cm)

OTHER METAL:
brass screws with rivets
copper headpins, 2
silver headpins, 2

JEWELRY TOOLKIT:
bracelet mandrel
butane torch
center punch tool
chemical brush
firing block
flat-nose pliers with protective handle
flux
plastic-coated flat-nose pliers
rawhide mallet
round-nose pliers
solder
wire cutters

SHAPING & FILING TOOLKIT:
metal bench block
metal file

BEADS & FINDINGS STASH:
bead cap, 5mm, 1
copper beads, 5mm, 2
cushion cut crystal, 5mm, 1
rhinestone chain

SAWING KIT:
drill and 1/16" bit
wood block

DARKENING & PATINAS TOOLKIT:
darkening solution

OTHER:
bowl and water
E6000 or other strong adhesive
steel wool
towel

TIPS

ETCHING THE CUFF

Because the surface of the cuff is curved, stamping will be a bit different. Instead of stamping directly onto the cuff, ink up your stamp and leave it on your work surface. Roll the cuff over the stamp. Proceed as usual, adding personal markings with a permanent marker if desired. Be sure to handle the cuff by the edges, as introducing oil to the metal will inhibit etching.

1 File Copper
File any rough edges on the copper using a metal file. Round the edges of the copper by filing them.

2 Drill Holes in Copper
Create one hole on each end of the sheet metal using a drill fitted with a 1⁄16" drill bit. File down any rough edges the drilling creates.

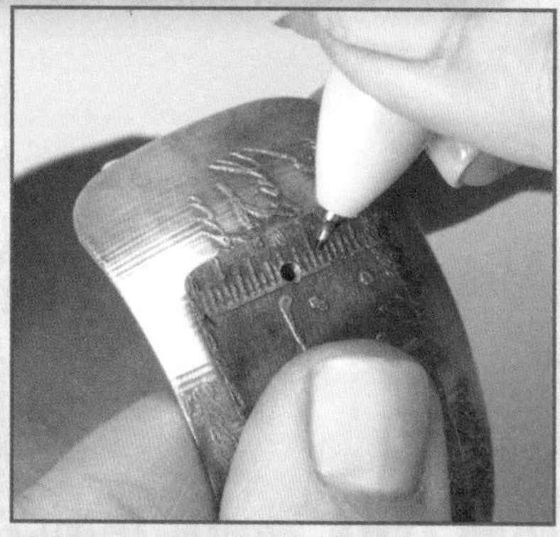

3 Mark Drill Holes on Cuff
Place the drilled copper piece on top of the cuff. With a permanent marker, create guides by marking through the drilled holes.

TIPS

CUFF TIP

If you are using a smaller cuff, be sure to adjust the width of the copper that will wrap over the top of the cuff. A perimeter of about ½" (13mm) should be left around the copper and exposing the cuff.

4 Prepare Cuff for Drilling
With a center punch tool, create a dimple on each marker guide.

5 Drill Holes in Cuff
Drill holes into the cuff using a drill fitted with a 1⁄16" drill bit. File down any protruding metal inside the cuff that results from drilling.

6 Shape Cuff
Put the cuff on the mandrel and press or squeeze it to reshape it to the desired size.

7 **Reshape Copper**
With a rawhide mallet and a bracelet mandrel, shape the copper until it easily conforms to the cuff.

8 **Attach Copper to Cuff**
Place the copper over the cuff and line up the drilled holes. Place one screw into each of the holes.

9 **Add Nut to Screw**
Add a nut to the screw on the back/inside of the cuff. Tighten the screw and nut. Repeat on the opposite end of the bracelet.

10 **Trim Excess From Screw**
Trim any excess metal from the screw using wire cutters. Tighten the nut even more and file the end until it is flush with the nut.

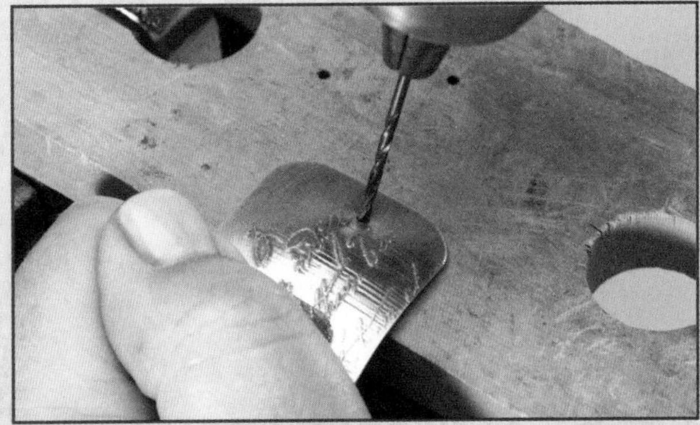

11 **Drill Additional Hole**
Drill an additional hole in the center of one end of the cuff. (A bead dangle will be attached using this hole.)

12 **Prepare to Solder**
Place the cuff on a firing block and use a brush to add flux to the area where the copper meets the brass.

13 Solder

Ignite the torch. Position the solder on the right side of the cuff, in the same area where the flux was applied. Holding the solder in one hand and the torch in the other, heat the solder. Once the flow of solder begins, place the solder over the seam of the copper and the cuff, moving it in a random manner. Repeat on the other side of the cuff.

Use coated flat-nose pliers to remove the cuff from the firing block. Place the soldered cuff in a bowl of water to quench it. Dry with a towel and buff with steel wool. Darken with solution if desired.

14 Attach Rhinestones

Attach a strand of rhinestones to the top edge of the cuff. Be sure to use an aggressive adhesive for best results.

15 Create and Attach Crystal Bead Dangle

Place a cushion crystal and a bead cap on a silver headpin. Create a loop in the headpin using the largest part of your round-nose pliers (see *Making a Wrapped Dangle*, page 16). Make two more dangles, this time using the copper beads.

Place the loop of each headpin through the loop created for the dangle. Place that large loop through the drilled hole in the cuff and wrap the loop closed.

SONGBIRD BIRDHOUSE NECKLACE

We all long for a lovely place to call home. Home beckons us when we are in far-away places; it offers comfort when we are feeling lost. Home is the place where our story begins and our tales forever live. The image of a birdhouse captures the sentiments we feel about our homes.

Songbird is full of symbolism and is a homage to that love of home; we hope that within your birdhouse you nestle your own sentiments and imagery, as this is the perfect project to turn into a statement piece.

You will find templates for *Songbird Birdhouse* on page 123. You can also print them out directly from the *Making Etched Metal Jewelry* companion page. Visit CreateMixedMedia.com/MEMJ-companion.

WHAT YOU'LL NEED

METAL, ETCHED AND RESHAPED:
copper, 24-gauge

nickel silver, 24-gauge

OTHER METAL:
brass headpin, 1

bronze wire, 22-gauge

copperwire, 20-gauge

gunmetal wire, 24-gauge

JEWELRY TOOLKIT:
bench block

butane torch

chain-nose pliers

circle cutter

firing block

flat-nose pliers

forming pliers

round-nose pliers

wire cutters

SAWING KIT:
drill and 1⁄16" bit

metal shears

wood block

SHAPING & FILING TOOLKIT:
jeweler's file

BEADS & FINDINGS STASH:
crystals, 2mm, 10

iridescent lavender coin pearls, 10mm, 3

pale pink potato pearls, 8mm, 2

pink potato pearls, 8mm, 2

rhinestone clasp

rhinestone rondelles, 5mm, 4

rhinestone rondelle, 7mm, 1

round crystals, 7mm, 8

DARKENING & PATINAS KIT:
darkening solution

OTHER:
dowel, ½" (13mm)

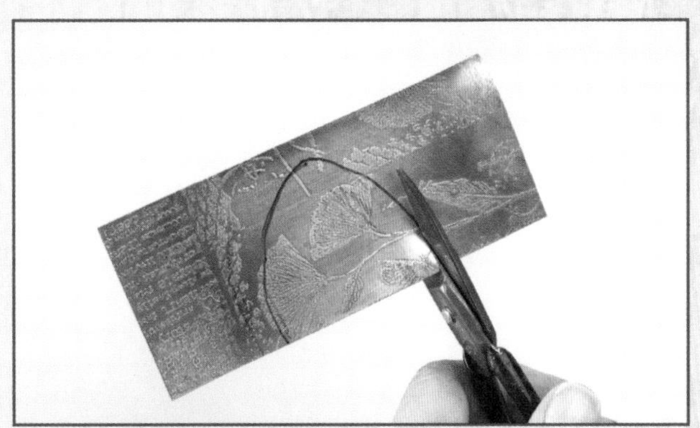

1 Cut Out Birdhouse Shape
Using the provided template, trace the shape of the birdhouse onto etched nickel silver. Use metal shears to cut out the shape. File any sharp edges and round corners.

2 Punch Center of Birdhouse
Use a circle cutter (see *Using a Circle Cutter*, page 18) to punch out the center of the birdhouse.

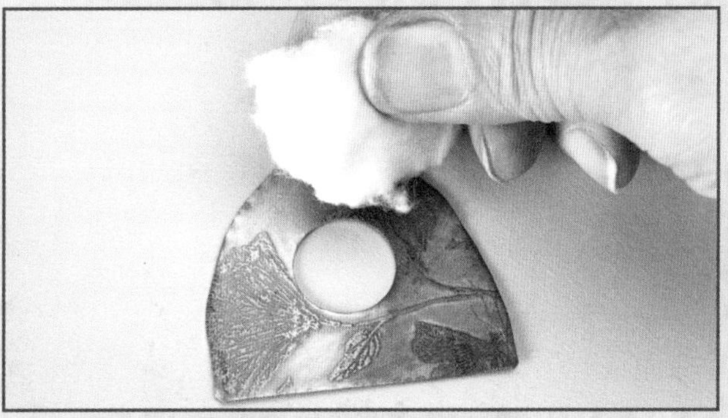

3 Darken Nickel Silver

Dip a cotton ball in darkening solution and apply it to the birdhouse shape. Allow the solution to dry and then buff the metal with steel wool to add depth.

4 Cut and Drill Copper Tab

Using the template provided for the back of the birdhouse, trace the shape onto the copper sheet metal. Cut out the shape with metal shears (the copper piece should measure 2½" × 1" (6cm × 25mm).

On one of the 1" (25mm) ends of the copper and using a drill fitted with a 1/16" drill bit, drill two holes, each about an ⅛" (3mm) from the edge of a 2½" (6cm) side.

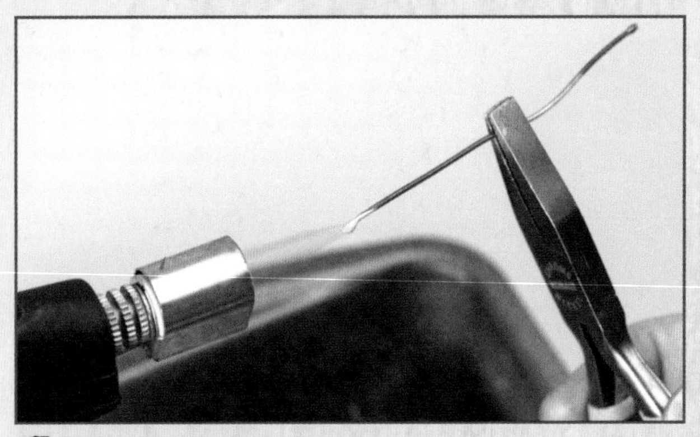

5 Make Headpins

Cut three 3" (8cm) pieces of 20-gauge copper and fire each with a butane torch until a ball forms (this is called drawing a bead). Make sure you hold the wire to the cone of the flame but not in it.

For this project, create double-headed headpins.

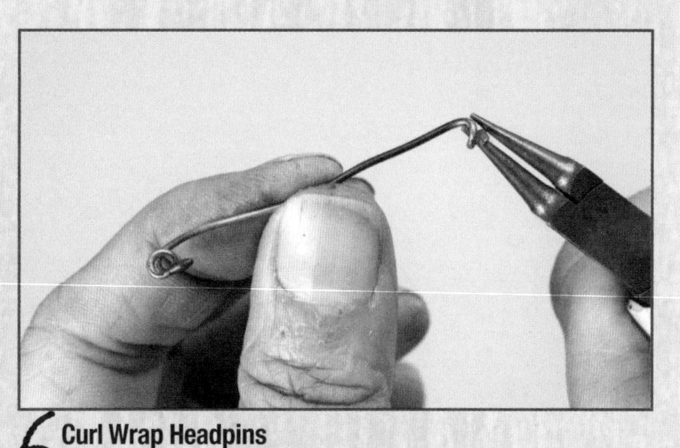

6 Curl Wrap Headpins

With round-nose pliers, hold the wire just beyond the ball and wrap the wire three times around the pliers.

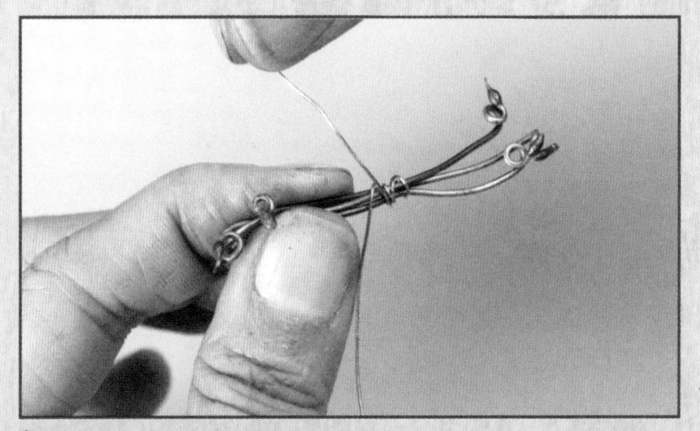

7 Bundle Curled Headpins

Bundle the the curled headpins and wrap a 12" (30cm) piece of 24-gauge brass wire three times around the center of the bundle, leaving a 1" (25mm) tail. Wrap the wire from the other end around the length of the bundle six more times and in a random fashion.

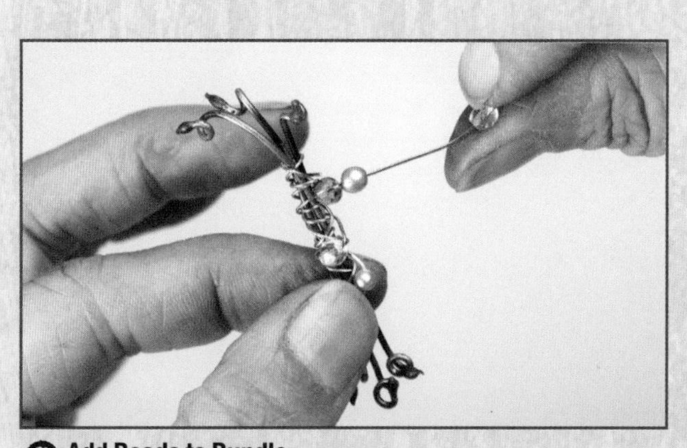

8 Add Beads to Bundle

Continue wrapping around the bundle, adding a 2mm to 3mm crystal or bead every few wraps until you achieve the desired look.

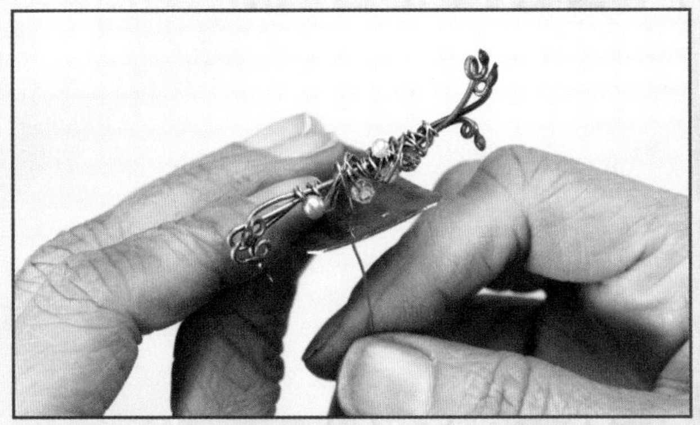

9 **Wrap Wire Into Copper**
When you have about 7" (13cm) of wire left, feed it into one of the holes in the copper tab.

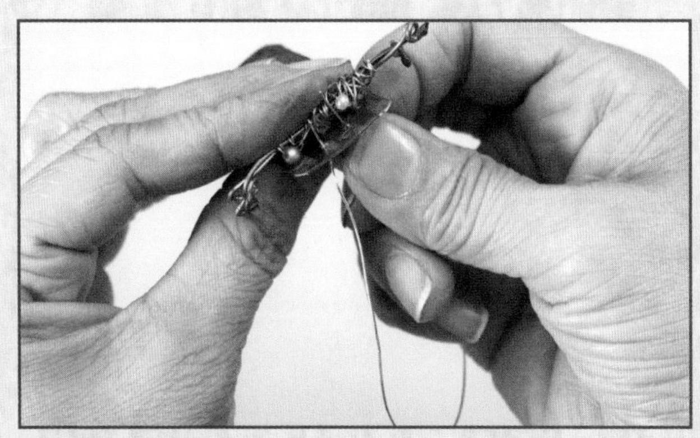

10 **Attach Bundle to Tab**
Bring the wire out the other hole. Then thread it back through the two holes four more times, catching the bundle in the wire each time.

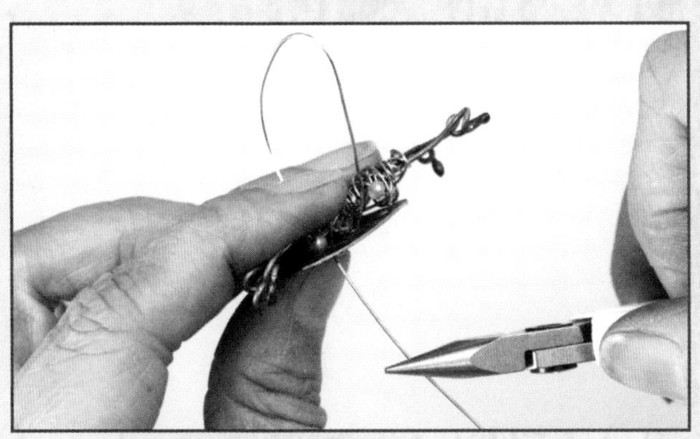

11 **Wrap and Cut**
Continue threading the wire around the bundle if it needs more security. Cut excess wire.

12 **Fold Tab**
Place the tab on a bench block with the bundle hanging over the edge by ½" (13mm). Gently bend the bundle tab over the edge of the bench block.

13 **Complete Tab Fold**
Use chain-nose pliers to help shape and refine the fold.

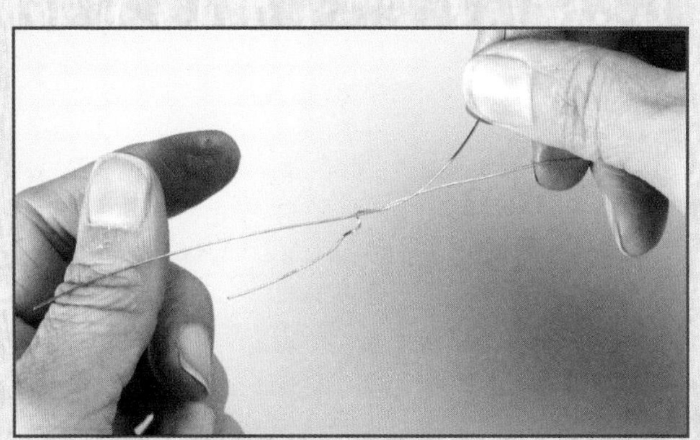

14 **Wrap Wires Together for Dangle**
Cut two 9" (23cm) pieces of 24-gauge brass. Cross the two wires and wrap one over the other for a length of just over 1" (25mm).

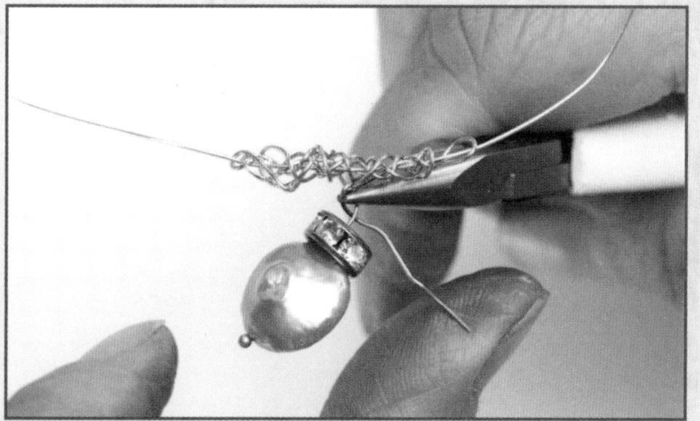

15 Continue to Wrap Wire

Back up and wrap over what you just wrapped. Continue this process of wrapping back and forth until all the wire has been used. Cut excess wire from the tail you have been wrapping. Slide a bead onto the other wire tail, loop and wrap the wire.

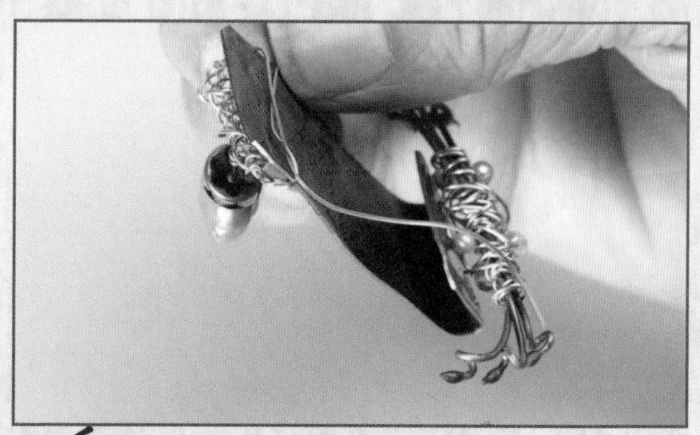

16 Attach Dangle to Copper Tab

Hold the wire-wrapped dangle against the front of the copper tab. Wrap the wire around the tab a couple of times.

17 Wrap and Tuck Remaining Wire

Once you feel the dangle has been secured to the copper tab, tuck the remaining wire into the existing wrapping. Trim any excess.

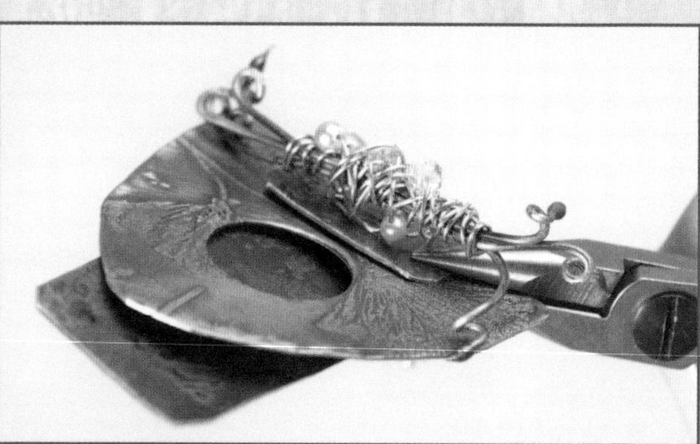

18 Insert Birdhouse Into Copper Tab

Slide the birdhouse into the copper tab and use pliers to tighten.

19 Trim Excess Copper

Cut off excess copper tab at the top of the birdhouse and file all edges to smooth.

20 Drill Holes at Top of Birdhouse

Drill five $\frac{1}{16}$" holes in a staggered row directly above the circle cut-out (see template for placement of drill guides).

21 Create Cupped Bead

Using a circle cutter, punch a small circle from a scrap of etched brass (see *Using a Circle Cutter*, page 18). Dome the circle (See *Using a Dapping Block/Doming a Circle*, page 18). You could use a purchased bead cup, if you prefer.

Cut a 14" (36cm) piece of 24-gauge brass wire, and draw a bead on one end. After the wire has cooled completely, slide a rondelle onto it and then the domed cup.

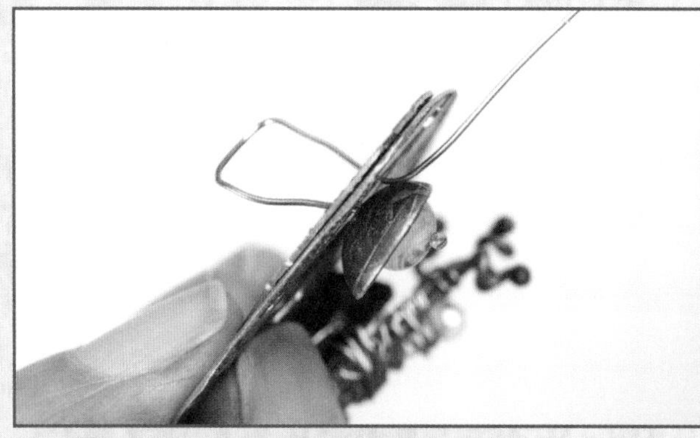

22 Begin Wrapping Wire to Secure

Thread the end of the wire through the second drilled hole from the left. Bring the wire back through the center drilled hole.

23 Continue Wrapping Wire

Alternate placing the wire through the second hole from the left, the center hole and the second hole from the right. As you do this,wrap the wire over the edge of the birdhouse twice on each side.

24 Finish Securing Bead Cup

Wrap the wire around the bead cup where it meets the birdhouse. Pull it through the center hole and wrap the end into the other wires there. Trim any excess wire.

25 Create Linked Chain (Right Side)

Cut fourteen 4" (10cm) pieces of 24-gauge gunmetal wire.

Using round-nose pliers, create a loop. Place the loop though the drilled hole on the left side of the birdhouse. Wrap the excess wire around the base of the loop and trim it. Slide one 7mm crystal onto the wire, create a second loop, wrap and trim the wire.

Using a second piece of 4" (10cm) wire, create a loop and place it through the last loop created. Wrap the wire to close the loop and trim any excess. Onto this wire, add one 10mm lavender coin pearl. Close the link. (See *Making a Wrapped Link/Wrapped Link Chain*, page 16.)

26 Continuing Chain

Continue building the chain by adding the following wrapped links:

- one crystal link
- one 5mm rondelle link
- one 8mm pale pink pearl link
- one 5mm rondelle link
- one 8mm pink pearl link
- one final crystal link

Do not wrap the second loop on the final link of the right side.

Create a similar chain on the left side of the birdhouse in the same manner. Turn the closing loop on this final link of the left side but do not wrap it.

27 Attach Clasp

Slide a head pin through the base of the rhinestone clasp. Onto the remaining wire, place one 7mm crystal, create a loop, wrap and close. Slide the loop onto the last loop of the last link on the right side. Wrap the loop to close and trim if necessary.

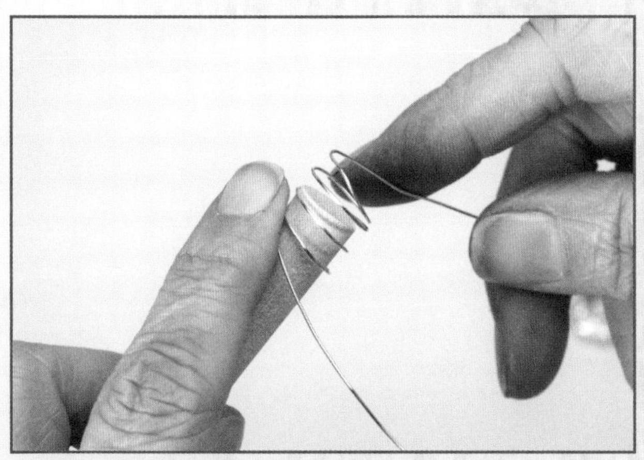

28 Create Eternity Links

Cut three 6" (15cm) pieces of 22-gauge brass wire. Wrap one piece of the wire around a ½" (13mm) dowel, leaving a ½" (13mm) tail on each end. Remove it from the dowel and compress the wire so it looks like a circle, then wrap the tails into the wire to secure them. Repeat to make a second link.

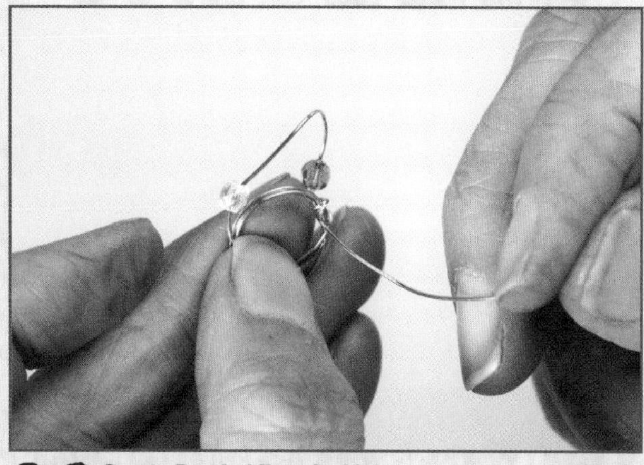

29 Create Beaded Eternity Link

Create a third eternity link following the instructions in step 28. However, during the wrapping process, slide three crystals onto the wire at random intervals. Wrap the wire until the link is completely closed.

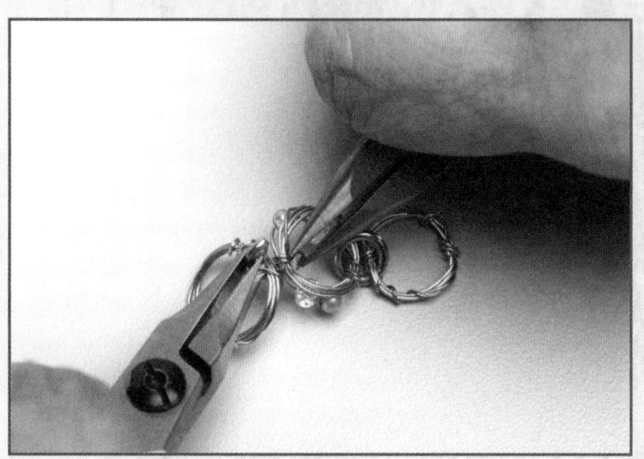

30 Join Eternity Links and Add to Chain

Join the links together with 5mm brass jump rings.

Slide one of the eternity links through the open link at the end of the left side of the chain. Wrap the loop to close.

SHE DREAMS JOURNAL

We are never too old to dream. Whether our dreams are about where we wish to travel or what we wish to create, dreams come from our hearts. In our view, dreams keep our souls happy and allow us the freedom to fall away from everyday life. Dreams afford us the freedom to escape into our very own place meant just for us.

When I came upon the idea for this journal, I was dreaming of fairy tales. I was intrigued by this fairy tale feeling. I wanted to create something usable but beautiful, something that could never be confused as utilitarian (but that was, really, utilitarian). Thus this journal was born. I can promise you the size of the book allows for a lot of sketching and writing, while the book's structure and adornments offer a bounty of beauty. Maybe it's the best of both our waking and dreaming lives.

You will find templates for *She Dreams* on page 123. You can also print them out directly from the *Making Etched Metal Jewelry* companion page. Visit CreateMixed Media.com/MEMJ-companion.

WHAT YOU'LL NEED

METAL, ETCHED AND RESHAPED:
copper, 24-gauge, 3½" × 3½" (9cm × 9cm)

nickel silver, 22 gauge, 3" × 2" (7½cm × 5cm)

brass, 22-gauge, 5" × 5½" (13cm × 14cm)

OTHER METAL:

steel jump rings, 19-gauge,10mm, 8

JEWELRY TOOLKIT:
ball-peen hammer

bench block

butane torch

circle punch

dapping block

firing block

flat-nose pliers

flux

flux brush

forming pliers

rawhide hammer

round-nose pliers

solder

wire cutters

SAWING KIT:
drill and 1⁄16" and 3⁄16" bits

jeweler's saw and #2 saw blade

metal shears

wood block

SHAPING & FILING TOOLKIT:
jeweler's file

steel wool

FABRIC & SEWING STASH:
cotton tapestry thread

embroidery floss

fabric doilies

interlining

natural cotton ribbon

osenberg fabric

raw silk ribbon

sewing machine

tapestry needle

thread

BEADS & FINDINGS STASH:
rhinestone strand

OTHER:
aquamarine dye

awl

binder clip

bone folder

bookbinding floss

bowl for water

brass eyelets, ⅛" (3mm), 4

carpet tacks

containers for dye

eyelet setter

leather punch tool

measuring spoons

permanent marker

ruler

tan dye

watercolor paper, 20" × 30" (51cm × 76cm), 300 lb. (640gsm)

Making the Body of the Journal

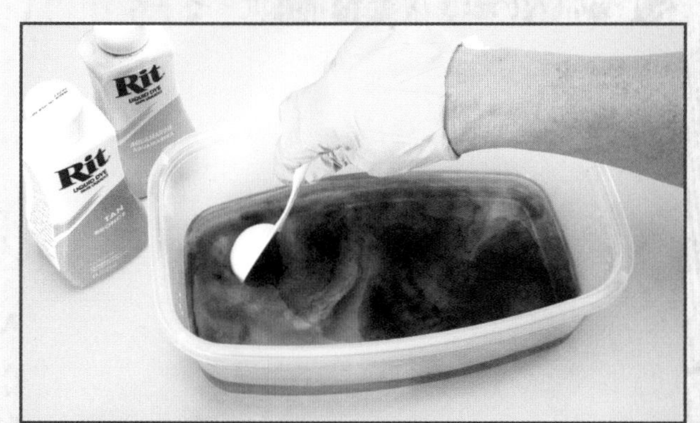

1 Mix Dye
Measure ½ teaspoon (2½ml) of aquamarine dye and ⅛ teaspoon (.5ml) of tan dye together with one cup of warm water in a plastic container. Stir to mix thoroughly.

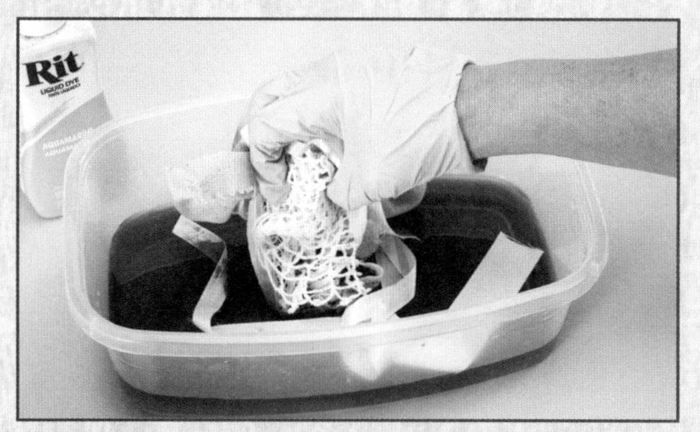

2 Dye Fabric
Place the osenberg fabric, lace and ribbon into the dye and leave them to process for five minutes. Then rinse the fabric, lace and ribbon with hot water and allow them to dry completely.

3 Cut Pieces for Signature Cover

Cut two pieces of dyed osenberg fabric to measure 6" × 5½" (15cm × 14cm) and one piece of interlining to 5½" × 5" (14cm × 13cm). Create a packet of the three pieces, with the interlining in the middle. (This will become the back cover for the journal.)

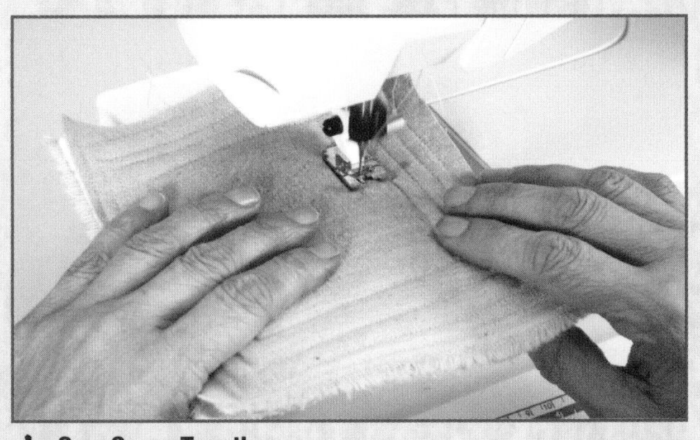

4 Sew Cover Together

Sew around the perimeter and then the interior, creating a quilted look. Sew a scrap to the center of the cover for decorative purposes if you'd like.

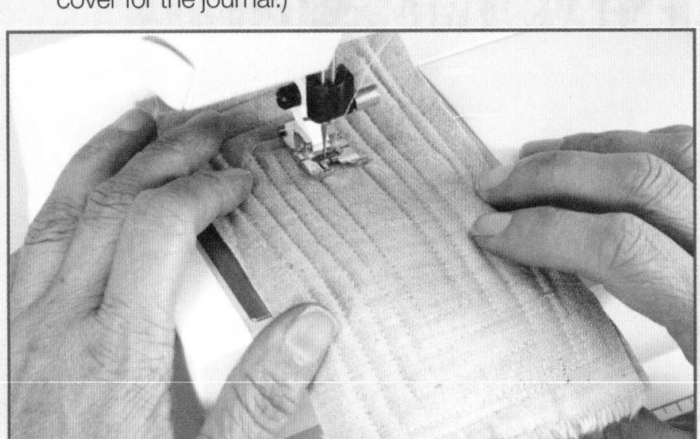

5 Cut and Sew Pieces for Spine

To create the spine of the book, cut two pieces of osenberg fabric to measure 3½" × 6" (9cm × 15cm), and one piece of interlining to 3" × 5½" (8cm × 14cm). Create a packet with the interlining in the middle and sew it together as you did in step 4.

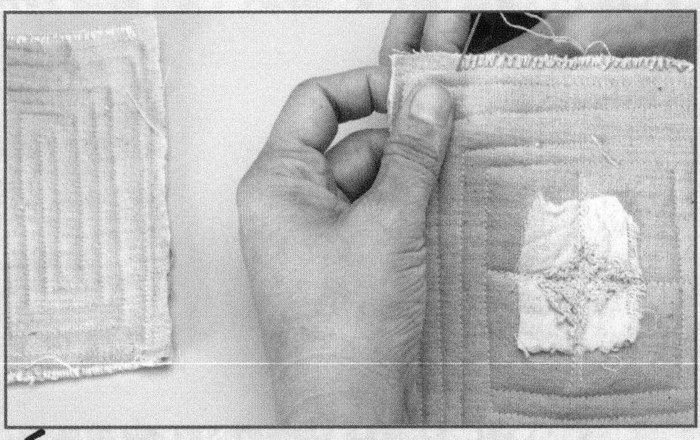

6 Stitch Edges of Cover and Spine

To secure and strengthen the pieces and for decorative purposes, hand stitch around the edges of both the cover and the spine.

7 Sew Spine to Cover

Using a couching stitch, sew the spine to the cover.

8 Create Book Signatures

Cut twenty-five pieces of 5" × 9" (13cm × 23cm) paper from the watercolor paper. Fold each piece of paper in half with a bone folder. Stack five folded pieces inside one another to form one signature. Secure pages with a binder clip to ensure consistent folding and to help the pages maintain their shape and position. Repeat with remaining paper to create a total of five signatures.

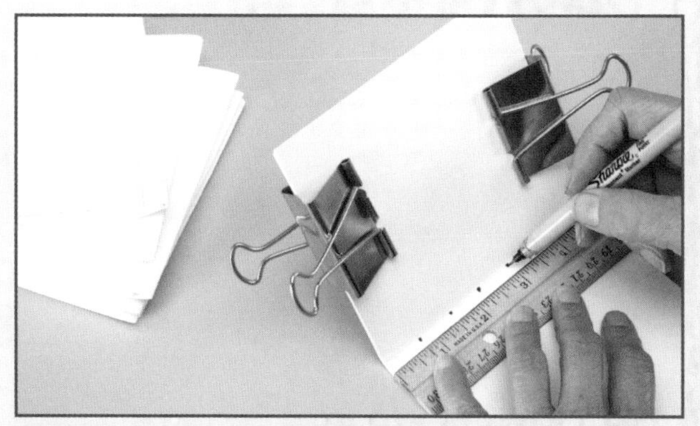

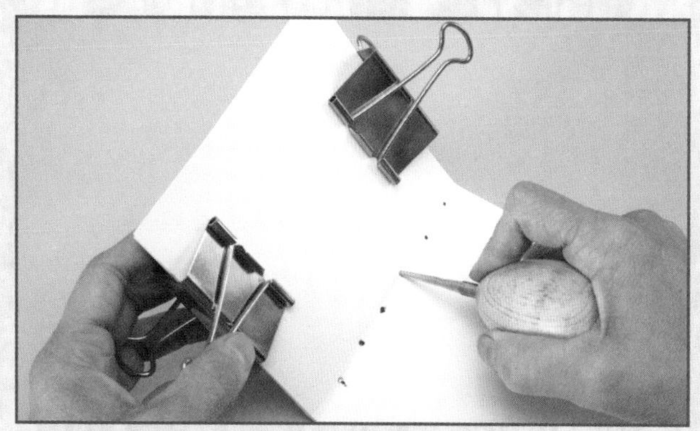

9 Add Needle Binding Guide Marks

Using a permanent marker, mark the paper along the inside fold of each signature. Place the marks every ¾" (19mm). There should be a total of six marks.

10 Punch Holes Through Guides

Push through the guide marks with an awl to create guide holes for the needle binding. Do this for all of the signatures.

11 Begin Needle Stitching the Signatures

Clip one signature to the fabric spine. Open to the center of the signature and push the awl through holes again to maximize guide space.

Measure a piece of wax linen that is four times the length of the book (approximately 24" [61cm]). Thread the needle with the wax linen, leaving a 2" (5cm) tail. Tie a knot in the end of the wax linen.

Starting from the inside of the signature, stitch out through the bottom hole. Then thread the needle into the signature through the next hole, out through the third hole, in the next hole, etc., until you bring the needle back into the signature through the sixth and final hole.

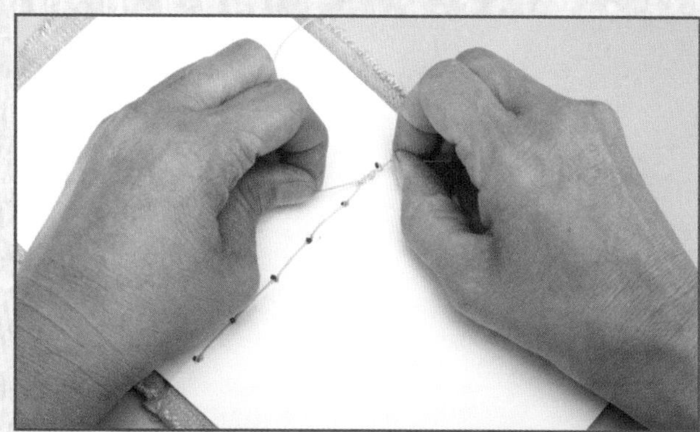

12 Continue Needle Binding

Work your way down through all the holes, starting by stitching out through the second hole from the top back. Continue until you have stitched back into the signature through the bottom hole.

13 Tie Off Binding

Tie the tail of the thread to complete the binding process.

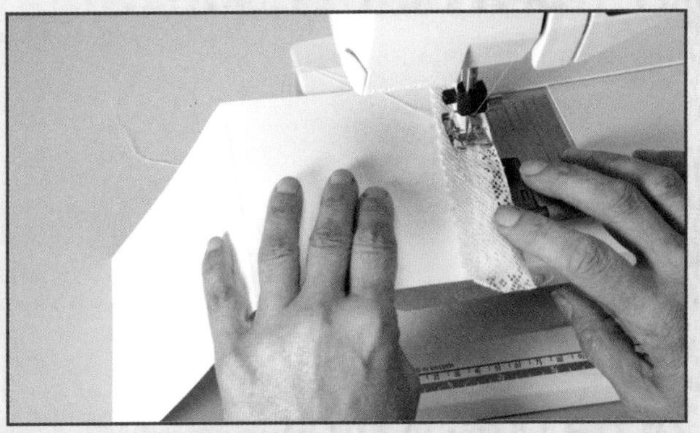

14 Sew Lace to Signatures

Sew one piece of lace or fabric to one page in each remaining signature. Overlap the lace so it hangs off the edge of the paper. If desired, you can ruffle the lace (see *Wrapped Treasures Fabric Tool Wrap*, page 119, step 16 for instructions on ruffling).

15 Needle Stitch Remaining Signatures to Spine

Repeat steps 11–13 for each of the remaining signatures.

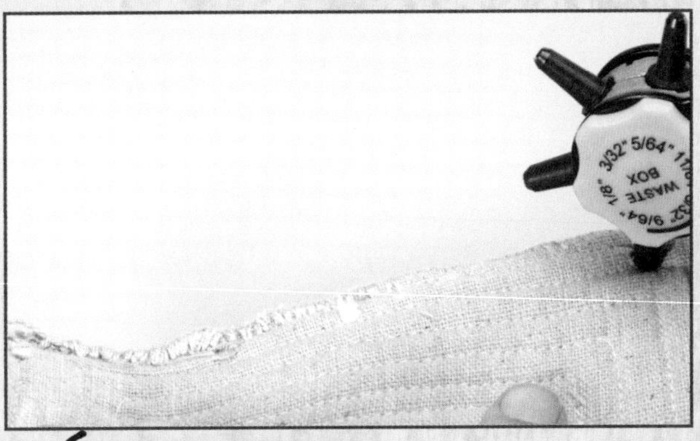

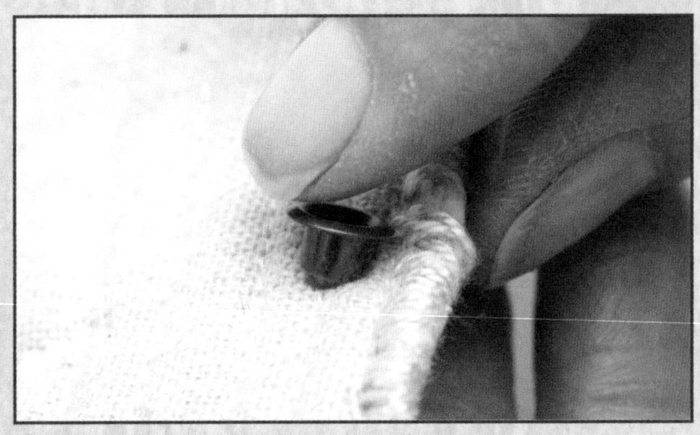

16 Punch Holes for Eyelets

With a leather punch tool set to ⅛" (3mm), punch three holes on the spine, starting 1" (25mm) from the top and then repeating every 1½" (4cm). These holes will bind the spine to the front cover.

Then, in the center of the outside edge of the cover, punch one hole. This hole will be used for the clasp.

17 Set Eyelets

Insert one ⅛" (3mm) eyelet Into each of the punched holes.

18 Close Eyelets

Using an eyelet tool and working on a bench block, hammer the eyelets to close them.

Making the Journal Cover

19 Patina Brass
Patina the etched brass using whichever method you prefer (see *Darkening and Adding Patinas*, page 20).

20 Mark Brass for Drilling
Using a permanent marker, create guide marks for drilling on the brass. The marks should line up with the eyelets you added to the spine.

21 Drill Holes in Book Cover
With a drill fitted with a 1/16" (2mm) drill bit, follow the marked guides to drill holes in the book cover.

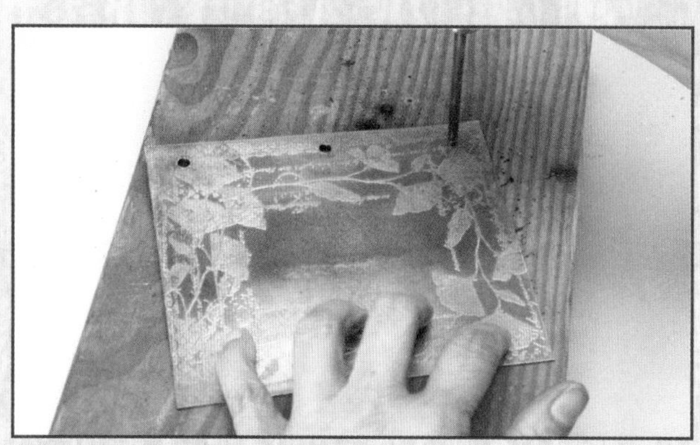

22 Enlarge Drilled Holes
To enlarge the holes, drill through them a second time using a 3/16" drill bit.

23 File Burrs and Rough Spots
Hammer away burrs resulting from drilling the holes and use a jeweler's file to smooth rough spots.

24 Clip Corners of Brass
Using metal shears, clip a *V* shape into one corner of the brass. Repeat this step for the remaining three corners. File the clipped edges to smooth them.

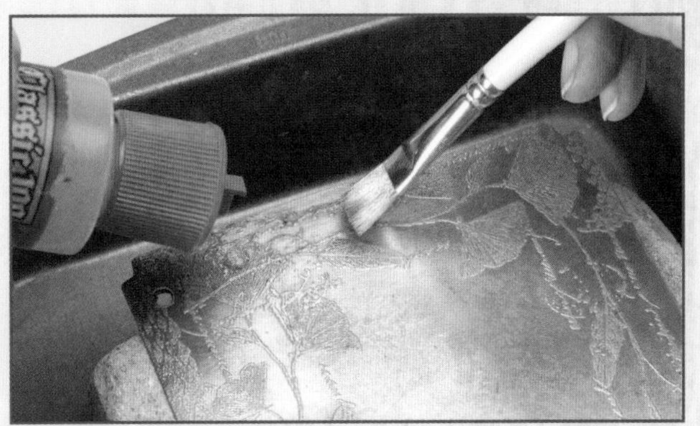

25 Apply Flux to Brass

With a flux brush, apply a thin layer of flux to the part of the brass to which you will adhere the rhinestone strand.

26 Apply Solder to Brass

Using a butane torch, apply a line of solder about ¼" (6mm) from the top edge of the brass.

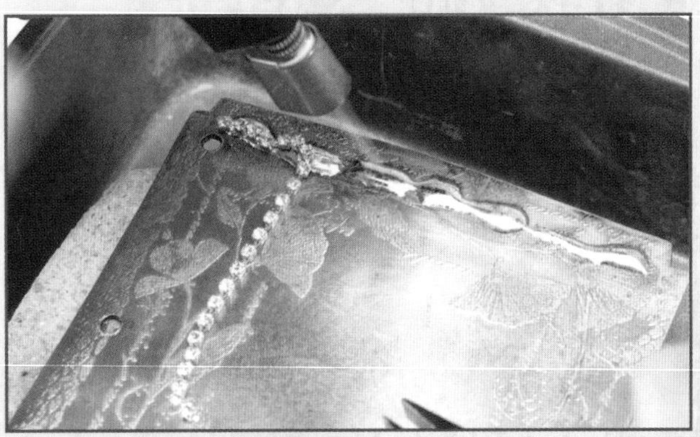

27 Embed Rhinestone Strand

Holding the rhinestone strand with safety pliers, reheat the solder with the butane torch. As the solder melts, embed the strand. Hold the strand in the flame for thirty seconds. Reheat more of the solder, and continue embedding the strand until all rhinestones are embedded. Let the solder and the embedded strand cool for one minute. Rinse the brass with soap and water and dry it with a soft towel.

28 Apply Darkening Solution

Add metal darkener around the embedded rhinestone strand using a cotton ball. Allow the solution to dry. Then buff the brass with steel wool to bring the etching to forefront.

29 Patina Etched Copper

Here we chose to go with the plant fertilizer patina method (see *Darkening and Adding Patinas*, page 21), because the green patina it creates on copper will look great with our finished project.

30 Cut Copper

Use shears to cut the copper using the provided template. Cut the corners and file the edges.

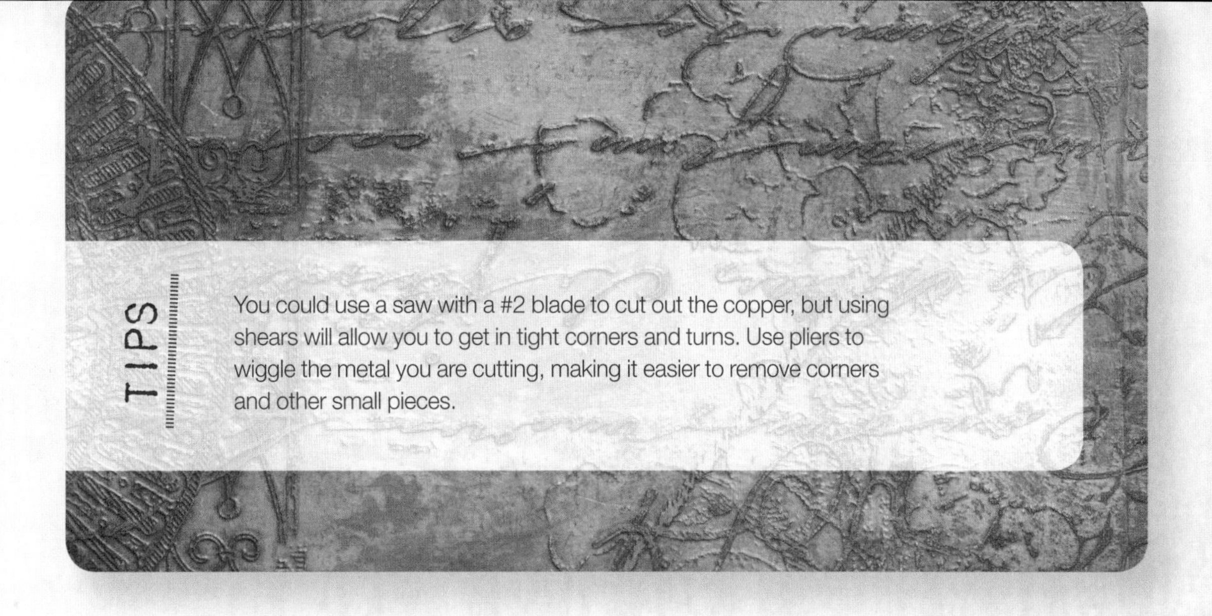

TIPS

You could use a saw with a #2 blade to cut out the copper, but using shears will allow you to get in tight corners and turns. Use pliers to wiggle the metal you are cutting, making it easier to remove corners and other small pieces.

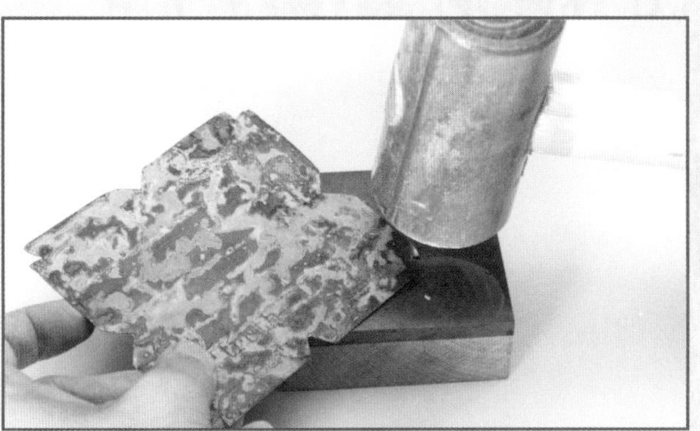

31 **Reshape Copper**
Use a rawhide hammer to flatten and reshape the copper.

32 **Drill Holes**
Use a binder clip to hold the etched nickel silver to the copper. With a permanent marker, create guides through which to drill holes.

Use a drill fitted with a 1⁄16" drill bit to drill holes though both the nickel silver and the copper.

33 **Stitch Nickel SIlver and Copper Together**
Place a few dyed fabric remnants between the nickel silver and the copper. With a tapestry needle and waxed linen, stitch the metal pieces together.

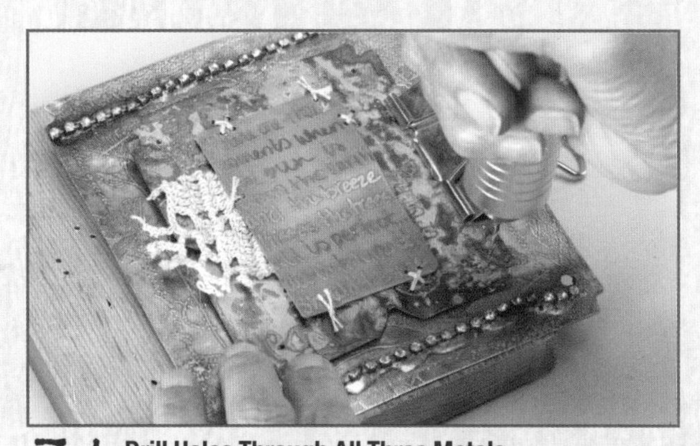

34 **Drill Holes Through All Three Metals**
Stack all three of pieces of metal together and secure them with a binder clip. With a drill fitted with a 1⁄16"drill bit, drill holes through all three layers. Enlarge the holes by redrilling them with a 3⁄16" drill bit.

35 Attach Metal Cover to Fabric Spine

Insert carpet tacks through each of the holes created in step 34. Use a hammer to guide the tacks and ensure they are flush against the copper.

Flip the metal over, and trim the stems of tacks to ⅛" (3mm) or less. (Do not trim the stems flush to the brass.)

36 File Ends of Carpet Tacks

Using a jeweler's file, file the sharp bits from the remaining stems of the carpet tacks.

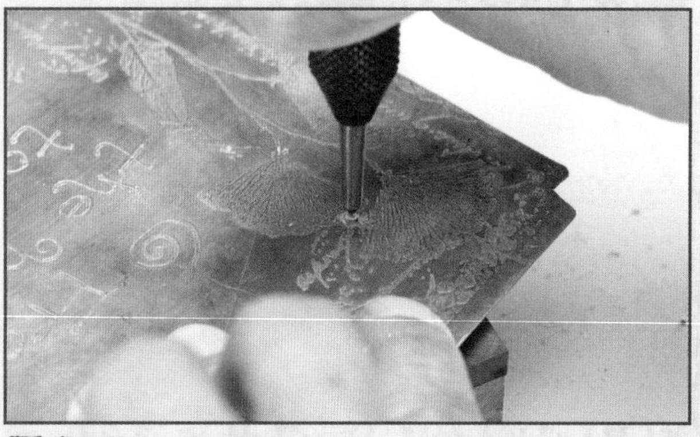

37 Dimple Tack Stems

With an awl and a hammer, create a dimple in each tack stem. Then hammer each so it is flush against the brass.

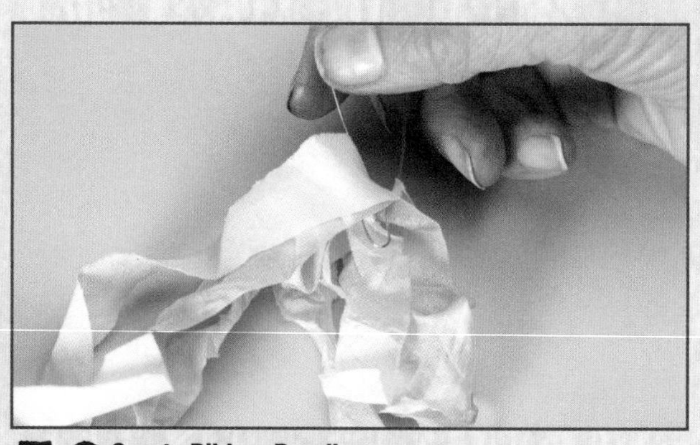

38 Create Ribbon Bundles

Layer together three 12" (30cm) pieces of ribbon. Cut 3" (8cm) of 24-gauge brass wire. Create a loop in the wire, and lay the ribbon within the loop. Do not close the loop. Repeat to make two more ribbon bundles for a total of three.

39 Attaching Cover and Spine

Place the metal cover on top of the signatures. Feed one of the ribbon bundles through the holes in the cover and spine, using the wire loop like a needle. Remove the wire.

40 Tie Ribbon and Repeat

Tie the ribbon bundle with a simple knot. Repeat steps 39–40 with the remaining ribbon bundles. Cover holes and spine eyelets.

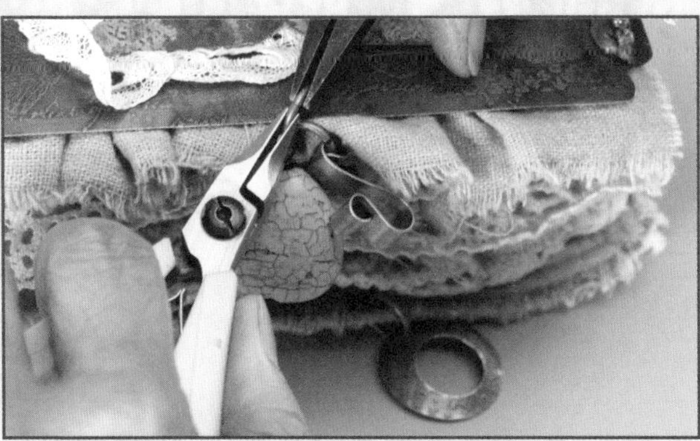

41 Embellish Ribbons

Add a variety of bead dangles and other embellishments to the ribbons. We used several of the beads featured in other projects, like simple dangles and more complex domed circles.

42 Create and Attach Clasp

Create a clasp to close your journal—we used the clasp featured in the Billowing "*S*" Links Bracelet project (see pages 52–53 for instructions). Embellish the clasp with bead dangles.

Using jump rings, attach the clasp through the remaining holes in the front and back covers.

TEMPLATES

Page 40
Page 46
Page 62
Page 46
Page 50
Page 84
Page 56
Page 88
Page 88
Page 88

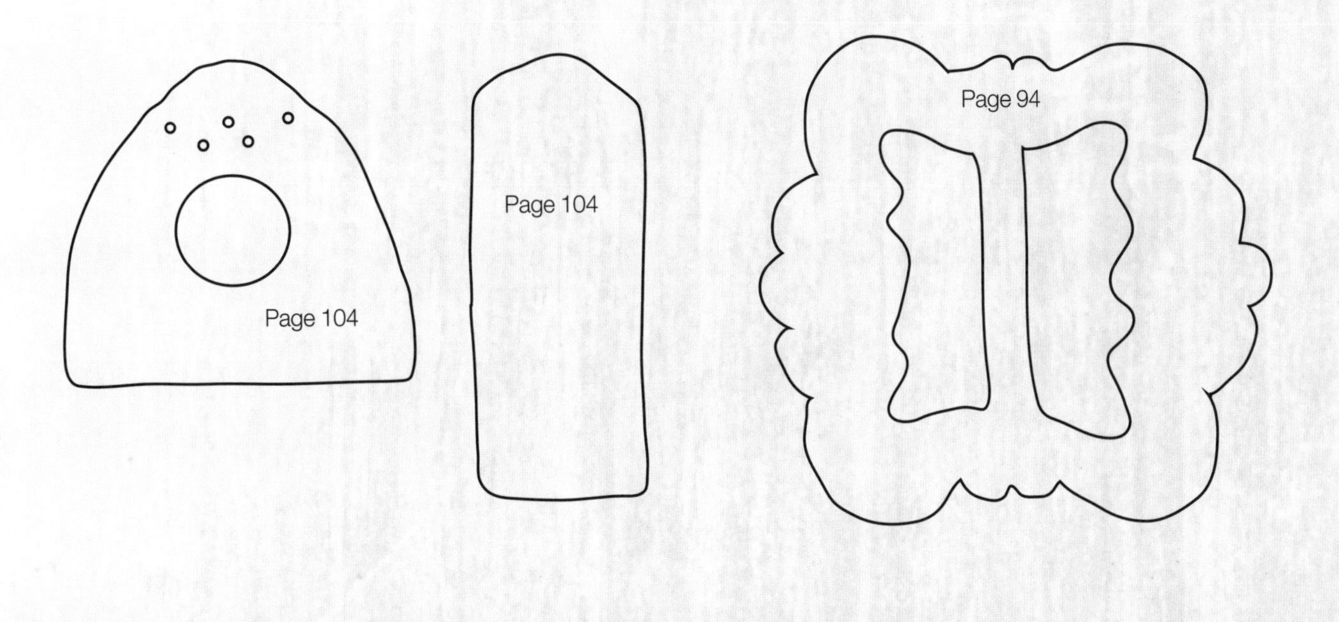
Page 104
Page 104
Page 94

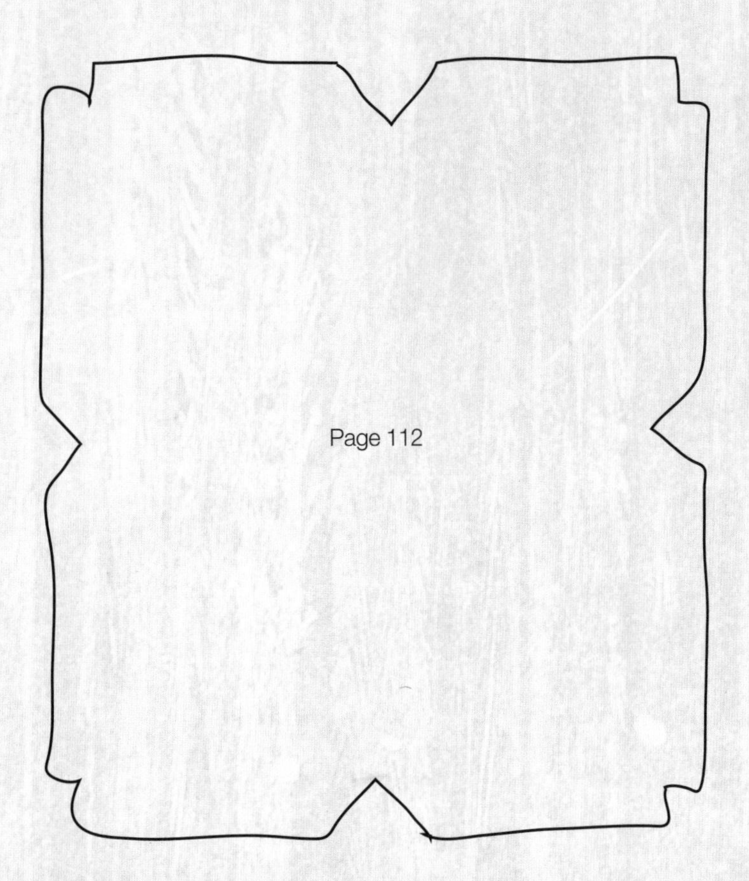
Page 112

RESOURCES

Back Porch Artessa
etsy.com/shop/TheBackPorchArtessa
rubber stamps

Connie Fox Tools
jatayu.com
pliers, wire cutters, metal punches, tools, supplies

Daniel Smith
danielsmith.com
ferric chloride

Darn Good Yarn
darngoodyarn.com
recycled sari silk, ribbon

Dick Blick
dickblick.com
rubber cement, transparencies, tracing paper

Eclectic Products
eclecticproducts.com
E-6000 adhesive

Gilder's Paste
gilderspaste.com
Gilder's Paste patinas

Gilding the Lily
vintagedesignresource.com
vintage chain, beads, pearls, metal darkening solution

Green Pepper Press
greenpepperpress.com
unmounted stamps

ICE Resin®
ICEResin.com
ICE Resin®, bezels, sheet metal, Kristen Robinson designer collection, rhinestones, micro nuts and screws

JewelryTools.com
jewelrytools.com
circle cutters, doming blocks, dappers

May Arts
mayarts.com
ribbon and fiber

Metalliferous
metalliferous.com
brass cuffs, bangles, sheet metal

Otto Frei
ottofrei.com
jewelry saws, bench pins, blade wax and blades

Ranger
rangerink.com
nonstick craft sheets

Rio Grande
riogrande.com
tools, tin snips, findings, wire, beads, pearls, beading cord and etching solution

Rockler Woodworking
rockler.com
Renaissance Wax (microcrystalline wax)

Sharpie
sharpie.com
permanent markers

Stampers Anonymous
stampersanonymous.com
rubber stamps

Stampington&Co
stampington.com
Love Lines rubber stamp set

Tsukineko
tsukineko.com
StazOn ink

Tweety Jill
tweetyjill.com
unmounted stamps

Volcano Arts
volcanoarts.com
soldering tools, solder, bookbinding materials, firing blocks, eyelet punch

INDEX

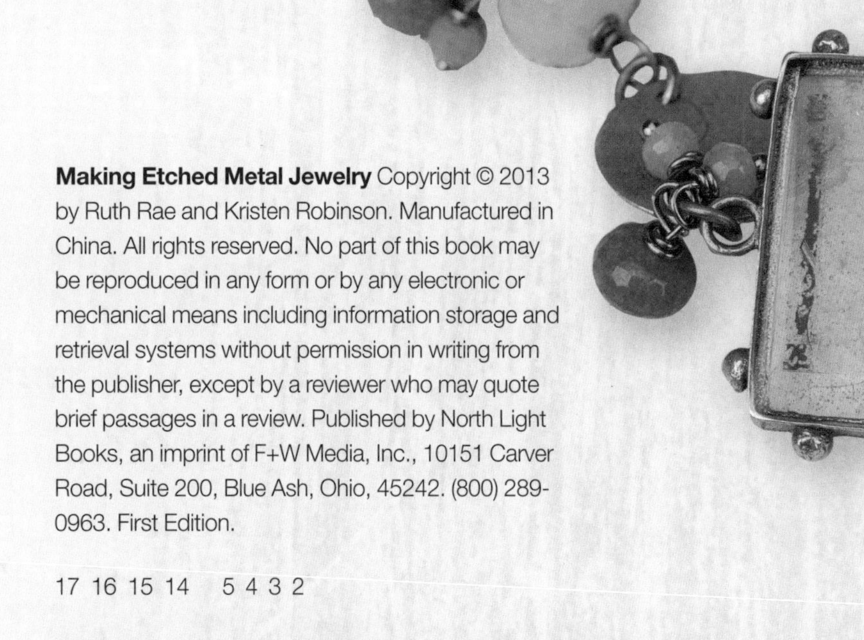

 Published by North Light Books, an imprint of F+W Media, Inc., 10151 Carver Road, Suite 200, Blue Ash, Ohio, 45242. (800) 289-0963. First Edition.

17 16 15 14 5 4 3 2

Distributed in Canada by Fraser Direct
100 Armstrong Avenue
Georgetown, ON, Canada L7G 5S4
Tel: (905) 877-4411

Distributed in the U.K. and Europe by F&W MEDIA INTERNATIONAL
Brunel House LTD, Newton Abbot, Devon, TQ12 4PU, ENGLAND
Tel: (+44) 1626 323200, Fax: (+44) 1626 323319
Email: enquiries@fwmedia.com

Distributed in Australia by Capricorn Link
P.O. Box 704, S. Windsor NSW, 2756 Australia
Tel: (02) 4560 1600
Fax: (02) 4577 5288
Email: books@capricornlink.com.au

ISBN-13: 978-1-4403-2705-6

fwmedia.com

EDITED BY Kristy Conlin

DESIGNED BY Geoff Raker

PHOTOGRAPHY BY Christine Polomsky and Corrie Schaffeld

PRODUCTION COORDINATED BY Greg Nock

METRIC CONVERSION CHART

to convert	to	multiply by
inches	centimeters	2.54
centimeters	inches	0.4
feet	centimeters	30.5
centimeters	feet	0.03
yards	meters	0.9
meters	yards	1.1

ABOUT KRISTEN ROBINSON

Kristen Robinson is on the artistic journey of her life, one she compares to dancing through the pages of a history book. With a love of all things from the past and the stories locked within them, she is drawn to many different forms of art, from jewelry and textiles to painting and collage. Kristen is the author of *Tales of Adornment: Techniques for Creating Resin Jewelry* and the designer of *Rue Romantique by Kristen Robinson*, a designer bezel collection from Ice Resin.

Kristen's art has appeared on the cover of an array of magazines, commercial art, stamp lines and DVDs. To learn more about her art and life, visit: *kristenrobinson.net*.

Dedications & Acknowledgments

I dedicate this book to my parents—Mom and Dad, without you I would never have dared to dream.

Travis and Conner, you make me what I am.

To my baby sister Heather, I adore you!

To my grandmothers, Lois, Pat and Fran, thank you for your strength and beauty.

It goes without saying that this book would not be what it is without my darling and dear friend Ruth by my side.

Kristy, you are the BEST!

Tonia, for seeing yet another idea for what it was—thank you!

Finally, to my Uncle Jim, who offers a bounty of inspiration, you have my deepest gratitude.

ABOUT RUTH RAE

Ruth Rae has an incredible talent for combining her deep love of treasures from the past with the cutting-edge trends of today. Ruth is known for her amazing jewelry creations, as well as mixed-media fabric work that combines textiles, words and found objects. Her artwork is recognized for its timeworn appearance, achieved through the layering of new and old, leaving the viewer feeling that they are taking in a creation from long ago.

Ruth's pieces have graced the covers and pages of many books and art publications, as well as DVDs and television. She aspires to motivate and inspire others to follow their dreams through both her artwork and teaching. To learn more about Ruth's art and life, visit: *ruthrae.com*.

Dedications & Acknowledgments

"Appreciation is a wonderful thing: It makes what is excellent in others belong to us as well."

—Voltaire

I dedicate this book to you, the creative explorers who like to expand and try out new things! And to my supportive family and friends for understanding and allowing me to be myself.

A heartfelt thanks to Kristen Robinson for reminding me that a little hard work only makes us stronger!

And a huge thanks to the North Light team for helping us turn our words and ideas into this book.